# Just jQuery
# Events, Async & AJAX

**Ian Elliot**

**I/O Press**
**I Programmer Library**

ISBN Paperback: 978-1871962529

First Edition
First Printing June, 2017
Revision 0

Published by IO Press          www.iopress.info
in association with I Programmer    www.i-programmer.info

# Preface

jQuery is the closest thing JavaScript has to a standard library, yet many programmers never venture beyond its most obvious facilities. As well as having easy to use and very powerful DOM manipulation features, described in the companion book ***Just jQuery: The Core UI***, it also offers an improved JavaScript event system, help with writing asynchronous code in the form of Promises, and easy to use and powerful AJAX functions.

While not every programmer will need these advanced features in the early stages of using JavaScript, they are unavoidable aspects of modern web programming and sooner or later you will find a need to master them all. jQuery is too good to turn down at any price, and the fact that it is free and open source makes it even better.

Of course a key advantage of using jQuery is that it covers up differences between a range of browsers and this means you can concentrate on writing your code and not worry about customizing for different browsers.

This book is specifically about how to make use of jQuery's event functions, Deferred and Promise functions and its AJAX functions.  It is about ideas. It does show you how to use jQuery, but mainly by explaining how jQuery approaches the task. Once you understand this there is little need to go over complicated examples where the problem is seeing the big ideas because the small detail is overwhelming. This is not a book of projects or case studies, it is about understanding jQuery.

In ***Just jQuery: The Core UI*** we looked at the basics of using jQuery as a way to work with, and generally manipulate, the DOM. Apart from a few introductory paragraphs in Chapter 1 there is very little overlap between the two books and, as long as you are confident about basic jQuery, you can skip the introduction.

Despite newer JavaScript frameworks and libraries gaining a disproportionate amount of attention, jQuery remains the most widely used JavaScript library. It is solid and dependable and has more to offer than most programmers, especially its detractors, know about. The purpose of this book is to explain how much it can help with some difficult tasks.

This two-book series is a revised and updated version of *Getting Started With jQuery* on the I Programmer website, www.i-programmer.info.

To keep informed about forthcoming titles visit the publisher's website:

www.iopress.info

This is where you will find errata and update information to keep up with changes in jQuery.

You can also provide feedback to help improve future editions.

## Table of Contents

**Chapter 11**
**Sending Data To The Client** 151

**Chapter 12**
**Transports And JSONP** 169

**Chapter 13**
**The jqXHR Object** 181

## Chapter 14
## Character Encoding      191

# Chapter 1

## Why jQuery for Events, Async & AJAX?

JavaScript is essentially an asynchronous language and you have to get used to this almost from the first instruction you write. What is less obvious at first is that asynchronous programs are more difficult to work with. First you meet the easy face of asynchronous programming – the event. You can't avoid using events in a JavaScript program.

**A JavaScript program is a collection of event handlers working to a common goal.**

We all learn to write event handlers very early on in our JavaScript education and we might even be told to keep them short. However, at first all event handlers are short because we are writing simple programs. Later things become more complicated and it comes as a painful lesson to many that you cannot simply stay in an event handler as long as you like. If you do, the UI (User Interface) will freeze and the user will assume your program has crashed. What is surprising is that there are no simple facilities to help you divide up your tasks into smaller units that don't swamp the UI activity.

## Why Asynchronous Code Is Needed

At this point you realize that there is more to asynchronous code, and events in particular, than meets the eye. It is time to dig a little deeper. Another aspect of slightly more advanced JavaScript websites is that they often need to load data into a page without having to reload the page. The big breakthrough technology in this area was AJAX, which introduces another element of asynchronous juggling.

The problem is that an AJAX request is nearly always asynchronous and your program has to wait for the file, or more generally the data you requested, to be ready for processing. You can't just wait for the data to arrive. You have to supply a callback function and then bring your code to an end. The callback function will be called when the data is available. In this sense it is much like an event, and you would suppose that there is nothing new, but callbacks are more difficult. The reason is that an event handler generally gets on with a job and doesn't have to interact with other parts of your code in an intricate way. A callback, however, is a continuation of part of your program. Some part of your program wanted some data and if it could be available immediately then it would have just continued on and processed it. The callback has to somehow pick up where your preceding code left off. This makes it more complex.

The big solution to this sort of problem is the Promise. This is was introduced in ES6 and isn't available on all browsers. A Promise is a way of organizing callbacks and while it isn't perfect it is better than nothing.

What all this means is that, as a competent JavaScript programmer, you have to deal with events, asynchronous code in general, Promises and AJAX and these are all sophisticated topics. Not only are they sophisticated there are variations in how they are implemented in different browsers. This is where jQuery comes into the story.

## jQuery Tools

In *Just jQuery: The Core UI* we looked at how jQuery provides powerful tools to let you work with the DOM and manipulate the UI directly. In this book the topic is the tools that jQuery provides for event handling, Promises and AJAX. These are often treated as secondary reasons for using jQuery because the DOM manipulation and UI aspects are often the headline reasons. However, jQuery provides an enhanced event handling framework, a standard Promise implementation, and a powerful and easy to use AJAX API. These are sufficient reasons for wanting to use jQuery and if you are already using jQuery for its UI abilities then it would be a shame to waste these "extras".

Currently jQuery 3 supports the following browsers:

**Desktop**

- Chrome: Current and previous version
- Edge: Current and previous version
- Firefox: Current and previous version
- Internet Explorer: 9+
- Safari: Current and previous version
- Opera: Current version

**Mobile**

- Stock browser on Android
- Safari on iOS

You can reasonably assume that everything described in this book will work on all of them unless otherwise mentioned.

## Event Handling

jQuery provides a much enhanced system of event handling that is uniform in syntax and behavior across all modern browsers and many legacy browsers. It provides a uniform way of attaching and detaching event handlers and it makes the order in which event handlers are called deterministic – they are called in the order they are attached – in contrast to the HTML standard which doesn't guarantee any particular order. In addition jQuery events have an improved delegation mechanism which makes it possible for a parent node to not just handle events that its children choose to handle, this is standard event bubbling, but to provide an event handler even if they don't have one – this is event delegation and only jQuery provides it.

It is more the case that jQuery re-implements the basic event handling system to make it more uniform and powerful, and this alone is a good reason to make use of it.

## Deferreds & Promises

jQuery introduced support for promises long before they were accepted into JavaScript as a standard feature. The penalty for being early is often getting it wrong and indeed early versions of jQuery didn't implement a version of the Promise that was as useful as it could be. Since Version 3, jQuery does offer a standard promise implementation while retaining many features of its original implementation. You will hear it said that there is no point in using jQuery for promises because JavaScript standard promises are superior. They may be superior but they are not supported on IE, including IE11 which is still a mainstream and widely-used browser.

jQuery implements promises using two distinct objects – the Deferred and the Promise. If you are simply consuming promises then you can ignore Deferred and nearly everything works like a standard JavaScript Promise, including under IE. If you want to add promise support to existing code then you will need to learn a little about Deferred as in many ways it makes implementing Promise support easier. It is arguable that learning about promise support via deferreds is easier than with standard promises and once you know how it works in jQuery it is easier to understand what is going on in JavaScript promises.

## AJAX

AJAX is in principle easy, but in practice it isn't. How AJAX works varies between browsers and jQuery smooths out these differences. It also extends what you can do with AJAX. There are several easy to use functions that implement the basic use cases, but there are also lower level facilities that allow you to implement your own special forms of AJAX using custom transports. The most important feature is that jQuery's implementation is promise-based and this makes it possible to write much higher quality AJAX code. It also provides data conversion utilities that can make your JSON into JavaScript objects and XML into XML objects. What you are getting is an easier to use and more powerful AJAX API that is very easy to extend.

## A Guide To This Book

As indicated in its title, There are three main themes in this book – events, asynchronous code and AJAX.

Chapters 2 and 3 deal with events in general and in particular. Here you will find out about what jQuery does to extend the event handling capabilities of JavaScript. Chapter 3 also deals with particular types of common event, mouse, keyboard and so on.

Chapters 4 thru 7 are about asynchronous code, which is a generalization of event handling. In Chapter 4 we learn about the problem of asynchronous code and how to convert long running event handlers into custom asynchronous code that doesn't hold up the UI. In Chapter 5 we learn how promises can make using asynchronous code easier. Chapter 6 digs deeper and explains how you can add promises to your own code both using jQuery's Deferred object and using the standard JavaScript Promise. We also look at how promises can be combined so that you can wait for all, one or any to complete and we look at the error handling capabilities of chained promises. Chapter 7 looks at how web workers can be used to implement real asynchronous code and how they can be used to relieve the pressure of long running code on the UI.

Chapters 8 thru 14 are all about AJAX. Here we work steadily through the jQuery AJAX facilities from the simplest to the most advanced. Chapter 8 starts off looking at the basic `get` and Chapter 9 looks at `post`. Then the next two chapters focus on the complementary tasks of getting data to the server and getting data back from the server. Chapter 12 looks at alternative transports and uses JSONP as its main example. Chapter 13 digs into the `jqXHR` object, which is the jQuery representation of the lower level browser AJAX interaction. Finally, in Chapter 14, we tackle the surprisingly difficult problem of using different character sets in both web page and AJAX interactions.

## Using jQuery

jQuery is just a JavaScript file that you have to load into any web page in which you want to use it. You can download it in either compressed or uncompressed form from the jQuery site. In most cases you want to use the compressed version, which is smaller and hence more efficient. The only reason for using the uncompressed version is if you want to look at the code for debugging reasons.

The compressed version is only 32KBytes which is usually small enough not to worry about. It is also likely that a user will already have a copy of jQuery in their browser cache and so generally it isn't downloaded on each use. There is also the slim build which leaves out the code that implements the AJAX component of jQuery. This only reduces the size of the compressed version by about 6KBytes and as a large part of this book is about using AJAX it is best to use the full version.

As an alternative to downloading and hosting the jQuery file, you can make use of a CDN – Content Delivery Network. A CDN is usually the best option because it usually offers a faster download to users and your server is relieved of the traffic. In addition, if your user has downloaded the same version of jQuery from the same CDN, then it will be used from the browser cache.

There is an official jQuery CDN hosted by MaxCDN and this is a good choice, but you can also opt to use Google, Microsoft, CDNJS or jsDelivr.

If you use the jQuery CDN you can also specify `integrity` and `crossorigin` attributes which the client browser will check to make sure that the code hasn't been tampered with.

For example, to include the uncompressed jQuery library for version 3.1.1 from the jQuery CDN you would use:

```
<script
   src="https://code.jquery.com/jquery-3.1.1.js"
   integrity="sha256-16cdPddA6VdVInumRGo6IbivbERE8p7CQR3HzTBuELA="
   crossorigin="anonymous">
</script>
```

This is the version used for all of the example code in this book. Of course, if you want to work with the latest version of jQuery then you might want to change the download link. However, for production code use a specific version of jQuery and don't upgrade the link until you have tested your code.

## How To Code

You can work with JavaScript and HTML using just a text editor, but there is a lot to be said for using a full IDE – Integrated Development Environment. There are many to choose from including WebStorm, Visual Studio Code, Aptana and more, but my own preferred IDE is NetBeans. This provides a good HTML/CSS and JavaScript editor and debugger. Using Chrome you can set breakpoints in JavaScript code and step through the code while examining the contents of variables. This is something that many IDEs offer, but what makes NetBeans so good is that you can also use it to develop server-side PHP and Java, and it will create a local copy of a website that you can use as a development server.

## Should I Bother Using jQuery?

You will hear comments that jQuery is not an essential component of web programming any longer. Part of the reason for this is that browsers are more standardized than before because of the introduction of HTML5, and partly because big frameworks like React or Angular.js make it redundant. Neither argument is 100% true.

The most important reason to use jQuery is that, while browsers are more conformant to standards, they are not perfect. Standards usually contain room for maneuver and interpretation and as a result you can still encounter small differences in browsers. Now consider what happens if you find such a difference – what are you to do? You could report a bug to the browser developers, but they might take the position that it is a feature rather than a bug, and that all the other browsers have implemented the specification incorrectly. However, if you use jQuery the chances are that it has already ironed out the difference. If it hasn't, then reporting the problem to the jQuery team will ensure that it is treated as a bug. The jQuery team regard any browser difference to be a problem that jQuery has to solve.

What about the framework argument? Yes, frameworks do make direct use of jQuery less important, although many are built on top of jQuery anyway. However, not all projects need the sophistication of a framework. What's more, a framework might well take you months to learn and master, only to discover that it doesn't quite do what you want; or the framework team might decide that they want to change direction, as happened with Angular.js and Angular 2. Using a framework isn't without cost and risk. For small projects, jQuery might provide all you need and it is still a good choice.

Finally jQuery is so common that it is regarded as JavaScript's standard library and, at 30Kbytes for a download, why not just use it?

## Summary

- jQuery is best known for its use in manipulating the DOM to create dynamic UI elements and this causes some of its best features – event handling, Promises and AJAX to be overlooked.

- jQuery re-implements the JavaScript event handling system to make it more uniform across browsers and to introduce significant enhancements.

- The Promise and Deferred objects in jQuery provide a standard implementation of the JavaScript Promise that works across many browsers that don't support the standard.

- The Promise object is all you have to know to make use of code that returns a Promise. The Deferred object is something you have to know about to implement code that returns a Promise object.

- You have to split any long running event handler code into small units which yield control back to the UI to keep it responsive. You can do this using custom asynchronous code or using web workers.

- jQuery introduces AJAX functions that work in the same way across browsers and it extends what you can do. The most important feature is that it is Promise based and this allows you to write modern AJAX code.

- It also provides facilitates to automatically convert data into more useful forms and to implement your own data transformation and transport functions.

- Although there are many libraries and frameworks vying for your attention there are few that are as solid and as useful as jQuery.

# Chapter 2

# Reinventing Events

JavaScript is an event driven language – which means you can't avoid dealing with events. jQuery doesn't just provide a browser-independent way of working with events, it reinvents the event system. With jQuery you really can write less and do more when it comes to events.

Events are central to JavaScript and to all JavaScript programs. You simply cannot afford to not fully understand them. In this chapter we introduce the idea of an event and an event handler and show how jQuery provides lots of help for you to make use of events and even extends the way events work.

First let's find out about how events work in pure JavaScript.

## Events

An event is something that happens at a particular time and at a particular location.

For example, the user might click a button or any element in the UI. Notice that an event is associated with a particular element. There isn't a single click event for the entire UI, but a click event can occur for every element in the UI that the user can click on.

You can associate a function, an event handler, with any event and the function will be called when the event occurs. This gives you the basic structure of a JavaScript program which is essentially a collection of event handlers.

The important thing to realize is that JavaScript is single-threaded. That is, there is only one thread of execution in a JavaScript program. This means that there is only one instruction being executed at any moment. But events can occur at any time so how do we cope with an event that occurs when the program is already doing something else?

What happens is that there is an event or dispatch queue to which the event is added until it can be dealt with. The system examines the dispatch queue and if there is an event waiting to be processed it takes it off the queue and calls the appropriate event handler. The event handler then runs to completion and only then does the system go back to the dispatch queue to see if there is another event to process.

Also notice that an event is only added to the dispatch queue if there is an event handler associated with it. Events that don't have handlers are simply thrown away.

## The JavaScript Way

The fact that JavaScript is single-threaded makes it very easy to reason about programs because two or more things cannot happen at any one time. In JavaScript only one thing is happening at any given time.

However, it also means that if you write an event handler that takes a long time to complete then nothing else can happen. To be specific, while an event handler is running no other event can be processed – they simply join the event queue - and the user is presented with a program that seems to be frozen.

**A JavaScript program is a collection of event handlers waiting for something to happen.**

The ideal JavaScript program doesn't do anything at all so allowing the system to wait for an event to enter the dispatch queue. This allows the system to respond to any user actions at once. The event handler that responds also does zero work and lets the system get back to waiting for the next event as quickly as possible. Anything that the program does simply slows the response to the user interface.

Of course this isn't possible because all programs actually have to do something to be useful. What you have to do is to keep in mind at all times that while your event handler is running the UI is frozen. Keep event handlers short, and if you can't you have to find other ways of either breaking up the computation or shifting it to another thread. It is also important to understand that it isn't so much the total amount of work that has to be minimized. What really matters is how often you yield control back to the system. You can get a lot of work done if you break it down into 50 millisecond chunks, for example.

These are topics discussed in later chapters.

## HTML Events

Now that we know how events and the dispatch queue work, it is time to look at how HTML events are implemented using just JavaScript - jQuery's improved event handling will be easier to appreciate when you know what it is replacing. In HTML you can set an event handler on an element using the well-known "on" attributes - e.g.

```
<button onclick="myEventHandler" ...
```

In code the modern way of doing the same job is to use the addEventListener method to register the event handler to the target.

For example:

```
button1.addEventListener("click",myEventHandler);
```

will result in myEventHandler being called when the user clicks the button.

Notice that while the HTML needs a string which provides the event handler's name, the addEventListener uses the reference to the function object. The first parameter specifies the event as a string. You can look up the names of all of the events in the documentation.

One small point that is often overlooked is that an event source can have more than one event handler registered with it.

For example,

```
button1.addEventListener("click",myEventHandler1);
button1.addEventListener("click",myEventHandler2);
function myEventHandler1(e){
 alert("event1");
}
function myEventHandler2(e){
 alert("event2");
}
```

when the button is clicked you will see two alerts, one per event handler. Notice that there is no guarantee as to the order in which the event handlers are called.

Why would you register multiple event handlers?

In many cases it doesn't make sense to use more than one event handler. The reason is that an event occurs and it is clear and simple what should happen. The user clicks a Save button and the click event should result in a click event handler being called that saves the data.

**One event – one handler.**

However, there are times when this isn't the case because an event is associated with multiple unrelated logical actions.

You might have a Save button that saves the data and incidentally shows the user an ad. In this case it makes sense to keep the functions separate. However, notice that there is no way to make sure that the ad is shown before the save or vice versa.

You can also remove an event handler using:

```
removeEventListener(type,function)
```

Notice that the type and function have to match exactly.

## Bubbling & Capture

We also have to consider the way events work in the DOM. In particular the way events "bubble".

In an HTML page different UI elements are nested inside one another. For example,

```
<div id="div1">
    Some Text
  <button id="button1">
    Click me
  </button>
</div>
```

defines a button contained inside a div. If we now define an event handler for each:

```
div1.addEventListener("click",myEventHandler1);
button1.addEventListener("click",myEventHandler2);

function myEventHandler1(e){
  alert("div");
}

function myEventHandler2(e){
  alert("button");
}
```

you can discover what happens when an event occurs on the inner UI element, i.e. the button.

With event bubbling the innermost item handles the event first and then passes it up in turn to the outer items. So if you click on the button you will see the button alert and then the div alert.

**Why do we want events to bubble?**

The reason is that there might be an action which has to be performed by the containing UI element when a child element is used. For example, the div event handler might reset all of the child buttons it contains. It might also be the case that you don't want to implement event handlers for all of the inner elements. In this case you could allow the event to bubble up to the outermost UI element and handle it there. Notice that the event object passed to the handler can be used to find out what UI element the event actually occurred on.

For example, if you define three buttons within a div you can handle a click on any button with an event handler registered to the div simply because the button click events bubble up:

```
<div id="div1">
<button id="button1">Click me</button>
<button id="button2">Click me</button>
<button id="button3">Click me</button>
</div>

<script>
 div1.addEventListener("click",myEventHandler1);

 function myEventHandler1(e){
   alert(e.target.id);
 }
</script>
```

When you click on any button the alert box correctly shows the id of the button.

**By default all events bubble up the UI hierarchy.**

The other way to allow events to propagate is called capture and this can be thought of as bubbling down – sometimes called trickling down.

In this case when an event occurs on an inner UI element it is the topmost enclosing UI element that gets to handle the event first.

To select capture you have to specify a third parameter – useCapture – when registering the event handler. So let's change the previous example of a button inside a div to use capture:

```
<div id="div1">
   Some Text
 <button id="button1">
  Click me
 </button>
</div>
```

```
<script>
div1.addEventListener("click",myEventHandler1,true);
button1.addEventListener("click",myEventHandler2);

function myEventHandler1(e){
   alert("div");
 }
function myEventHandler2(e){
   alert("button");
 }
</script>
```

Notice that the div event handler is now registered with useCapture set to true. This means that all click events that occur on UI elements that are contained by it are handled by it and then passed down through  child elements back to the element that the event occurred on. Now if you click on the button you will see the div message first and the button message second.

In most cases it is much simpler to use bubbling because older browsers don't support capture.

## Basic jQuery Events – on, off, one

Event handling in older browsers is a mess.

You can spend a lot of time trying to write event handling code that works as widely as possible but it is better to simply give in and use jQuery which smooths out the differences. jQuery also more or less re-implements the event handling system to make is more logical and more powerful.

It is important to realize the jQuery really is re implementing the event handling system, and this means that it works in ways that are different from the browser's native event handling and even from the W3C events specification.

In jQuery you register an event handler using on and remove an event handler using off. These are the only two functions you need but there are others that add some versatility. Versions of jQuery before 3 made use of a set of now deprecated functions – you can ignore these.

The on function has the basic form:

`.on(events,selector,data,handler)`

where selector and data are optional and both are described in detail later in the chapter. As always jQuery will work out which parameters you have omitted by their type.

The simplest use of the on function is to attach a handler to an element:

`$("#button1").on("click",myEventHandler);`

This attaches myEventHandler to the element with id button1. Of course, if you select multiple elements the same event handler is attached to them all.

If you want to set multiple events in one operation you can use an alternative version of on:

```
.on(eventsList,selector,data)
```

In this case the first parameter is an object of key/value pairs. The keys are events and the values are event handlers.

For example:

```
$("#button1").on({
          click:myEventHandler,
          dbclick:myEventHandler2
        });
```

sets two event handlers one for a click and one for a double-click.

Notice that if you set multiple event handlers on an element then they will be called in the order in which they were added. This is, of course, different to raw JavaScript events where the order is undefined.

jQuery also allows you to add the same function as an event handler on the same element more than once. This too is different to raw JavaScript events where multiple copies of the same event handler are simply discarded. Having multiple copies of the same function means you can trigger the action more than once for each event and you can also pass different parameters if you want to – see later.

Another jQuery extension to event handling is the one function. This works like on, but any event handler you add using it will only be triggered once on each element it has been added to.

For example if you use:

```
$("#button1").one("click",myEventHandler);
```

then the event handler is added as before, but now it will only be called once. That is, the user can only click the button and trigger the event handler once.

You can remove an event handler using the off function.

If you want to remove a specific event handler use:

```
.off(events,selector,handler);
```

which will remove the handler that was added using the same event, selector and handler.

If you want to remove a set of event handlers you can pass an object of key/value pairs with the key being the event name and the value being the event handler to remove.

```
.off(events,selector);
```

Finally if you want to remove all event handlers for a specific event use:

```
.off("event");
```

and to remove all events from an element use:

```
.off();
```

For example, to remove the click event handler given earlier, use

```
$("#button1").off("click",myEventHandler);
```

To remove all click event handlers, use

```
$("#button1").off("click");
```

and to remove all event handlers of any type, use

```
$("#button1").off();
```

This is all you need to know about adding and removing events at the basic level but we need to fill out details of how the selector is used to specify delegated events and how to implement custom events – see later.

## The Event Handler

When an event handler is called in response to an event it is passed some parameters that help it work with the event. Standard JavaScript event handlers are passed an Event object which has properties determined by the type of event. jQuery provides its own Event object which is a "normalized" version of the raw JavaScript event object.

That is, the jQuery event object provides the same information independent of the browser in use. You can access the native event object via the originalEvent property and this is sometimes necessary for events that provide additional information.

In addition to the Event parameter the event handler is also provided with the element that the event occurred on as this. Notice that this is a raw DOM Element and if you want to use it as a jQuery object you will need to wrap it in $(this).

There are a lot of possible event properties that you could work with depending on the type of event but there are a few that are common to all events.

These are briefly described below, although a full explanation is postponed until a later section.

- There is a set of properties that tell you about the type of event and the element it occurred on:

    **event.type**

    gives the name of the event for example "click".

    **event.namespace**

    gives the namespace that was specified when the event was triggered. This is covered in the section on custom events.

    **event.timeStamp**

    The time that the event occurred measured in milliseconds from January 1,1970.

    **event.data**

    An object of custom data passed to the event handler. This is another jQuery extension of the basic event handling mechanism.

- There are a set of properties concerned with the way the event bubbles:

    **event.target**

    This is the element that the event occurred on i.e. the element that the user actually clicked on. This is always the deepest or innermost element of a nested set of elements. Notice that because of event bubbling this isn't always the same as the element the event was added to.

    **event.currentTarget**

    The element that the bubbling phase has reached.

    **event.delegateTarget**

    The element that the event handler was attached to.

    **event.relatedTarget**

    Any element that is also involved in the event. This is only supplied for events where there is another element involved. For example, when a mouseout event occurs the relatedTarget is the element the mouse pointer entering.

### event.result

The last value returned by an event handler.Finally there are some properties that relate to mouse and keyboard:

### event.pageX

The mouse position relative to the left edge of the document

### event.pageY

The mouse position relative to the top edge of the document

### event.which

The key or mouse button that was pressed when the event occurred. This is a replacement for event.keyCode and event.charCode provided by jQuery to make working with the mouse and keyboard easier. For a mouse event 1= left button, 2=middle and 3=right button. Note that scroll wheel is usually a middle button.

### event.metaKey

True if a meta key - the Windows or Mac Command Key was pressed when the event occurred.

Many events have a default action. For example clicking on a link loads that page into the browser. You can stop default actions using:

```
event.preventDefault();
```

You can discover if some other event handler had prevented the default action using:

```
event.isDefaultPrevented();
```

You can also stop bubbling, see later using either:

```
event.stopPropagation()
```

or:

```
event.stopImmediatePropagation();
```

and you can test to see if bubbling has been stopped using:

```
event.isPropagationStopped();
```

See the section on bubbling and delegation for more information.

# Event Data

Perhaps the most useful addition that jQuery makes to the event handling mechanism is the ability to pass custom data to an event handler. If you include an object of data as the second or third parameter in on or one, then that object will be passed to the event handler in the data property of the event object.

The key point is that the link to the object is live. The object is set at the time that the event handler is attached, but what matters is the state of the object when the event happens.

For example:

```
mydata={};
mydata.value=10;

$("button").on("click",mydata,
            function(event){
                            alert(event.data.value);
                         });
mydata.value=20;
```

What value do you see when the button is clicked?

The answer is that the event is almost certain to happen well after the code shown has completed and hence the value stored in the object is 20.

Notice that this implies that the mydata object still exists even though the code that created it came to an end well before the event handler was called. The reason that mydata still exists is that a closure is formed because the event handling function persists after the code has completed. This is an important general point and applies to all event handlers. As they persist for the time that they are attached to an element, they are always associated with a closure that provides them with access to all of the variables that were in scope when they were defined.

For example, suppose we create a function to attach the event handler:

```
mydata={};
mydata.value=10;
setEvent=function(){
            $("button").on("click",mydata,
                        function(event){
                                alert(event.data.value);
                             });
            };
setEvent();
mydata.value=20;
```

In this case the result is exactly the same in that mydata.value is set to 20 before the event handling function is called. However, if we move the definition of mydata into the setEvent function:

```
setEvent=function(){
                    var mydata={};
                    mydata.value=10;
                    $("button").on("click",mydata,
                                       function(event){
                                         alert(event.data.value);
                                       });
                };
setEvent();
mydata.value=20;
```

Then the value passed to the event handler is 10 because the mydata outside of the setEvent function is a different object i.e. it is not local to the function. In fact if mydata is defined outside of the function as well, the attempt to set the value causes a runtime error. This emphasizes the fact that a closure is in operation.

In fact because of the closure we don't really need the data parameter to pass data to the event handler. For example:

```
setEvent = function () {
                    var mydata = {};
                    mydata.value = 10;
                    $("button").on("click",
                                       function (event) {
                                         alert(mydata.value);
                                       });
                };
setEvent();
```

Notice that we don't need the event object at all as mydata in the closure.

You might at this point think that there is no advantage to using event.data but this overlooks one difference between it and simply using the closure. The object reference is stored and if you change the object reference later the event handler still gets the original object. For example:

```
setEvent = function () {
                    var mydata = {};
                    mydata.value = 10;
                    $("button").on("click",mydata,
                                       function (event) {
                                         alert(event.data.value);
                                       });
                    mydata={};
                };
setEvent();
```

Notice now that mydata is an empty object at the time the event handler is called but the event handler still gets the original object with value set to 10. This wouldn't work if you just used the closure.

This may seem to be a slight difference but sometimes it can be important. For example a standard demonstration of how things can go wrong with a closure is to try to capture each of the values in a for loop:

```
for(i=0;i<5;i++){
            $("button").on("click",i,
                        function(event){
                                alert(event.data);
                        });
        }
```

In this case the index i is the object, remember nearly everything in JavaScript is an object. If you run this and click the button the five event handlers will be called in order and you will see 0, 1, 2, 3, 4 displayed.

Compare this to:

```
for(i=0;i<5;i++){
            $("button").on("click",
                        function(event){
                            alert(i);
                        });
        }
```

where the closure is used to access the variable i which is 5 when the loop ends and this is what each of the event handlers access.

A subtle difference that probably needs some thinking about to get straight in your mind.

## Custom Events

jQuery makes it very easy for you to fire an existing event or implement your own custom event. The `trigger` function will execute all event handlers attached to an element.

```
trigger(event,parameters)
```

where event is the name of the event you want to trigger or an event object specifying the event. The second parameter is optional, but if used it provides additional parameters to pass to the event handler. Notice these have nothing to do with the data passed in the on function and retrieved via the event.data property. These really are additional parameters to be passed to the handler. If parameters is an object then it is passed as a single extra parameter. If parameters is an array then each element is passed as a parameter.

For example to fire a click event on a button you would use:

```
$("button").trigger("click");
```

In this case the event handlers are executed in their standard order and passed the data object specified in the on function when they were attached to the button.

You can specify additional parameters as part of a standard event handler like click but notice that when the event is fired in the usual way i.e. not via trigger, these additional parameters will be undefined.

For example:

```
$("button").on("click",
                function(event,param1,param2){
                        alert(param1 + param2);
                });
```

```
$("button").trigger("click",["first","second"]);
```

In this case param1 is set to "first" and param2 is set to "second" but if you click on the button then they are undefined. Notice that the extra parameters always come after the default event parameter.

You can use trigger to implement your own events. All you have to do is decide on a name for your event and use on to attach an event handler for it. For example, to attach myevent you would use:

```
$("button").on("myevent",
                function(event,param1,param2){
                        alert(param1 + param2);
                });
```

Which also passes two additional parameters as in the previous click example. Now you can trigger your custom event using:

```
$("button").trigger("myevent",["first","second"]);
```

It is usually a good idea to use a name space to make clear that your event belongs to you. A name space is just a dot separated name. For example:

```
myevent.mycompany
```

You can have multiple name spaces but these are not hierarchical.

For example:

```
myevent.myname.mycompany
```

creates two name spaces myname and mycompany and you can refer to the event as:

```
myevent.myname
```

or:

```
myevent.mycompany
```

If you add an event with a name space you can also make use of the name space removal feature in the off function. So:

```
.off("myevent.myname")
```

would remove all myevents attached using the myname namespace.

This works even with standard events such as click.

The jQuery event system is very general and it even works with standard JavaScript and DOM objects. For example:

```
var obj=$({}).on("myevent",
                function(event,param1,param2){
                        alert(param1 + param2);
                });

obj.trigger("myevent",["first","second"]);
```

In this case the event handler is attached to the empty object and we trigger the same event on that object.

Not only will trigger fire event handlers that you have attached to an object, it will also attempt to run properties with the correct name as functions.

If an object has a property that is the same name as the event then it will be run as a method i.e. without any event parameters. If an object has a property that has "on" in front of the event name then this will be run as an event handler. That is, it will be called with an event object and any custom parameters you might have defined.

This calling of properties can be useful but it can also cause problems. To avoid calling any properties that might have the same name as an event you can use the triggerHandler function in place of trigger.

Notice that triggerHandler will not call any methods called event but will call any methods called onevent as event handlers. It also only operates on the first element of any list of matched elements. Also it doesn't bubble events, see later, and it returns the last event handler's result, not a jQuery object.

The main use of custom events is to provide an organized way of passing information about the state of any custom component you might implement. For example, you might implement a custom dataChange event if your component is updated by the user or an outside entity. This would allow a programmer using your component to write code that could react to the change without having to get involved in the internals of your component. Custom events can also be useful in JavaScript libraries that don't implement a UI. For example you could have an event that indicated an error condition or that something was complete in an object that implemented some numerical procedure.

# Bubbling & Delegation

We have already discussed the idea of event bubbling in the context of the DOM. jQuery takes this a little further. You can use the selector part of the on function call to control the way that an event handler behaves during event bubbling.

If you don't specify a selector then you get the classical bubbling behavior. That is the event handler is attached to each element in the jQuery results. It is fired when an event occurs on that element or bubbles up to that element as a result of an event on a child element.

To illustrate this we can re-implement the earlier example but using jQuery:

```
<div id="div1">
Some Text
 <button id="button1">
 Click me
 </button>
</div>

$("#div1").on("click",function(){alert("div");});
$("#button1").on("click",function(){alert("button");});
```

If you click on the button then you will see the button message followed by the div as the event bubbles up. If you click on the div you will only see the div message.

We can use this to find out about the information about the event passed in the event object:

```
$("#div1").on("click",
                function(event){
                    alert($(event.target).attr("id"));
                });

$("#button1").on("click",
                function(event){
                    alert($(event.target).attr("id"));
                });
```

Now if you click in the button you will see the button1 message twice once from the button's event handler and once from the div's event handler. The target is the button in both cases.

If you change the code to:

```
$("#div1").on("click",
              function(event){
                  alert($(event.currentTarget).attr("id"));
              });
$("#button1").on("click",
              function(event){
                  alert($(event.currentTarget).attr("id"));
              });
```

you will see button1 followed div1 as currentTarget gives the element that is attached to the event handler invoked by the bubbling.

Notice that you can stop bubbling by calling the event object's stopPropagation or by just returning false. Notice that this doesn't stop any other event handlers on the same element from running - just the bubbling of the event. If you want to stop everything after the current handler, other event handlers and bubbling, then use stopImmediatePropagation. Notice that this is the only way to stop event handlers on the same element from running. The reason is that the list of handlers to run is constructed when the event occurs and, if you remove an event using off, this does not remove it from the list of event handlers to run. The removal will only have an effect when the event next occurs.

This is just standard HTML event bubbling implemented by jQuery. If you specify a selector then you get something different. What happens is that if a child element matches the selector then the parent will provide the event handler for the event. This is called a delegated event handler. Notice that, unlike the default bubbling, the child element doesn't have an event handler of its own.

An example will help make delegation clear:

```
$("#div1").on("click","button",
                function(event){
                    alert($(event.currentTarget).attr("id"));
                });
```

Notice that now we have specified a selector "button". This means that any event that occurs on a button that is contained within the div will be handled by the event handler. Now if you click on the button you will see the button1 message and no div1 message. What might be more surprising is that you don't see anything if you click on the div.

In this case the div's event handler is only handling events on any button objects the div contains.

This is a particularly useful feature if you plan to dynamically add elements into the container because the event handler will be called for events on elements that didn't exist when it was attached to the container.

It is fairly easy to understand how delegation works. When you click on the button it doesn't have an event handler attached so no event handler is called but the event still bubbles up to the div. At this point jQuery intercepts it and check to see if there is a delegated event handler that matches the event and the element that the event occurred on. If so the delegated event handler is called.

You also need to know that in this case target is button1, currentTarget is the element that the delegated event is handling i.e. button1, and delegateTarget is the element that the handler is actually attached to i.e. div1.

Also notice that this is the same as target for direct and delegated events.

## Summary

- An event is something that happens to a particular element in the UI.
- JavaScript is single threaded and only one instruction is being obeyed at any given movement.
- If an event handler runs for too long then the UI thread cannot handle other events and the user interface seems to freeze.
- You can add an event handler using addEventListener in JavaScript.
- HTML events bubble up from the element that the event occurred on to the parent elements that contain it.
- jQuery re-implements the event system adding many improvements.
- You can attach an event handler using on, remove it using off, and attach it for a single event using one.
- jQuery creates a uniform event object to pass to event handlers.
- One of the most useful improvements in the event system is the ability to pass data to the event handler.
- You can create custom events using trigger and fire built in events under program control.
- jQuery supports bubbling and adds delegation where an element that doesn't have an event handler can pass the event to a parent element which does have an event handler.

# Chapter 3

# Working With Events

jQuery provides both a general framework for handling events and event-specific functions. While you can use the general functions – on, off and one - to deal with all events, the event-specific functions do focus the mind on how events are used and are worth knowing about.

Events are central to the way we program in JavaScript. A JavaScript program is essentially a collection of event handlers. In this chapter we take a closer look at the different types of event you are likely to encounter and in particular the events that jQuery thinks are important enough to be worth having special functions for, in addition to the general purpose on, off and one, which switch an event on just once.

There are five categories of event:

- Mouse
- Keyboard
- Form
- Browser
- Document

Keep in mind that all of these functions are equivalent to using on with the name of the event. This means that events that are attached using these functions can be manipulated as if they had been added using on. For example they can be removed using off.

## Mouse Events

### Click

Mouse events are the ones we use most. The first example of an event most people are introduced to is the mouse click event. However, the mouse can be a difficult input device to get right.

The most basic mouse event is the click, and you can attach a handler to any element using:

```
click(eventdata, handler)
```

where eventdata is optional and is an object that is passed to the handler when it is fired.

You can also fire the click event on an element by using:

```
click()
```

i.e. with no parameters.

All of the specific event functions work in the same way – only the name of the event and function changes.

For example:

```
$("#button1").click(
            function(event){
                console.log("Button1 clicked");
            });
```

We are so familiar with the click event that we often don't bother to find out exactly what a click is. To register a click the left mouse button has to to be pressed down and released while the mouse pointer is inside the element that registers the click.  What this means is that you can abort a click by moving outside of the element before you release the button.

There are lower level mouse event handlers, mousedown and mouseup, which are fired when a mouse button is pressed and when released respectively. A mousedown and a mouseup event occur before a click event.

A click event handler will be called when a user taps on a touch device and so it is fairly safe to use.

## Double Click

There is also the double click event and dblclick function that can be used to attach a handler in much the same way:

```
$("#button1").dblclick(
            function(event){
                console.log("Button1 double clicked ");
            });
```

In this case the surprise might be that you can double-click a button. It may be allowed but it isn't used very often. In fact as the double click generally means "open me" or "run me" it tends to only be used on elements that can be opened or run.

A double click is slightly more complicated than a click because there is a system specific delay between clicks. The double click event is fired when the user clicks twice on an element within a given time. As for a click the pointer has to remain inside the element the entire time.

Double clicks are best avoided if you want your program to work on a mobile device. The reason is that there is no direct equivalent to the double click. A single tap may be treated as a click but a double tap is not and in fact double tapping is a very rare gesture on a touch-enabled app. If you really must have a double click working on a mobile device then you will need to write something at a lower level and this is difficult to get working across devices.

Another problem is that browsers differ in the way they handle click and double click handlers bound to the same device – some fire two click events before the double click and some just one.

Finally, notice that click and double click only work with the mouse's primary button – usually the left button. Some browsers did fire a click event for other buttons but this is not now standard behavior.

If click and double click is only for the primary button, what about the middle/scroll wheel and the right button?

## Right Click

The right button is associated with the context menu and so its event is called contextmenu:

```
$("#button1").contextmenu(
                function(event){
                  console.log("Button1 right clicked ";
                });
```

The event will only fire if the button is right clicked. The event handler will be called, but when it has finished the context menu will be displayed. To suppress the context menu you need to add a call to preventDefault:

```
$("#button1").contextmenu(
                function(event){
                  console.log("Button1 right clicked ");
                  event.preventDefault();
                });
```

Long touch events are generally translated to right clicks, i.e. they display the context menu on a mobile device. For this reason using right click is relatively safe.

## mouseup and mousedown

The middle button or scroll wheel doesn't have a special event handler in jQuery and only recently has there been a standard for its use. If you want to work with the scroll button then look up the "wheel" event.

If you want to respond to left, middle and right clicks then you have no choice but to program your own. The lower level events mousedown and mouseup are fired when any mouse button is used and you can discover which button was pressed using the which property of the event object, which is 1 for the left button, 2 for the middle button and 3 for the right button.

For example:

```
$("#button1").mousedown(
                    function(event){
                        console.log("Button1 down "+event.which);
                        event.preventDefault();
                    });
```

in this case you will see 1,2 or 3 displayed depending on which button you press.

You can use mousedown and mouseup to synthesize a click event on any button, however, it isn't quite as easy as you might think. If you want to make a proper click event then you have to make sure that the mouseup happens on the same element that the mousedown occurred on. One way of doing this is:

```
var clickdown=function (event) {
                event.preventDefault();
                var target = event.target;
                $(document).on("mouseup",
                                function (event) {
                                  if (target === clickdown.target){
                                      console.log("click "+
                                                        event.which);
                                  }
                                  $(document).off("mouseup");
                                });
            };
```

What is happening here is that when the mousedown event occurs the element that it occurred on is stored in the local variable target. Then the function sets a mouseup event handler on the document. Any mouseup event that occurs will bubble up to the top level document and we can check using target, which is available to the handler due to closure, that the event did occur on the same element.

To use this click function all you have to do is:

```
$("#button1").mousedown(clickdown);
```

Notice that the actual event handler, i.e. the code that does something useful, is defined on the mouseup handler.

## Mouse Location Events

A set of events is provided to let you respond to a mouse's location. Notice that none of these events have good equivalent gestures on a mobile or touch device and hence they are best avoided.

### mouseenter and mouseleave

Are triggered when the mouse pointer enters and leaves an element respectively. This event doesn't bubble so the mouse entering and leaving a child element does not fire the event on the element containing the child.

### mouseover and mouseout

Are triggered when the mouse pointer enters and leaves an element respectively. They are bubbling versions of mouseenter and mouseleave. This means that the events will be fired if the mouse pointer enters or leaves a child element of the element the handler is bound to.

To see the difference use something like:

```
<div id="outer">
Outer
 <div id="inner">
Inner
 </div>
</div>
```

and

```
$("#outer").mouseover(
                function () {
                  console.log("enter");
                });
```

You will see the event triggered if the mouse moves over the inner or outer div. If you change mouseover to mouseenter you will only see the event when the mouse moves over the inner element.

### hover

Hover will bind one or two handlers to the mouseenter and mouseleave events. If you specify two functions then the first is bound to mouseenter and the second to mouseleave. If you specify a single function then it is bound to both events.

### mousemove

This event is fired every time the mouse moves within the element the handler is bound to. You can obtain the mouse's position from the pageX and pageY properties of the event object. These give the position relative to the top left-hand corner of the page. The only problem with using this event is that it is fired every time the mouse moves and this can be a performance issue. Any event handler you bind to it should finish as quickly as possible.

As an example of mousemove, let's implement a "scribble" application. In this case all we have to do is draw a dot at the current mouse position as it moves. To do this we can use a canvas element:

```
<canvas id="Canvas"
  width="600" height="600"
  style="height:600px;width:600px;">
</canvas>
```

The program is:

```
$(document).mousemove(
              function (event) {
                var c = $("#Canvas");
                var ctx = c[0].getContext("2d" );
                ctx.fillStyle = "rgb(200,0,0)";
                ctx.fillRect(event.pageX, event.pageY, 1, 1);
              });
```

If you try this out you should be able to draw on the page

If you change mousemove to mousedown then you will only be able to draw at each mousedown event.

# Drag and Drop

One of the standard compound gestures you will encounter on the desktop UI is drag and drop. This is far less commonly used in a web page and hardly used on mobiles. For this reason you might want to avoid its use.

It is a compound gesture because it involves a sequence of events. First we have a mousedown event on the object to be dragged. After this the mousemove is used to track where the object is being dragged to, and the object is dropped at that location when a mouseup event occurs.

The only difficult thing about drag and drop is deciding how to implement it. You can use basic HTML and JavaScript to implement it; you can use jQuery UI, which has a browser independent implementation; or you can use the HTML 5 drag and drop facilities.

It is interesting to see how drag and drop is implemented in the most basic way. Let's drag and drop a button:

```
<button id="button1"> drag me</button>
```

First we have to make sure that the button's positioning is set to absolute and we need two variables to record if a drag is in progress and which element is being dragged:

```
var drag = false;
var target;
$("#button1").css("position", "absolute");
```

When the mouse button goes down on an element all we have to do is remember the target and set drag to true:

```
$(document).mousedown(
            function (event) {
              drag = true;
              target = $(event.target);
            });
```

Notice that we save the target as a jQuery object.

The mousemove event handler simply has to update the target's position, but only if drag is true:

```
$(document).mousemove(
            function (event) {
              if (drag) {
                target.css("top", event.pageY)
                      .css("left", event.pageX);
              }
            });
```

You can modify the mousemove to move a graphic, a bounding rectangle say, that will stand in for a complex element that is too slow to redraw at each move.

The drop action is implemented as a mouseup event and in this case all it has to do is set drag to false and set the final position of the object:

```
$(document).mouseup(
            function (event) {
                if (drag) {
                    drag = false;
                    target.css("top", event.pageY)
                            .css("left", event.pageX);
                }
            });
```

You also need to check that a drag is in progress as there is no point in doing anything unless it is. The drop routine is usually more complicated because of the need to do different things depending on what the drop target is. For example if the button was dropped on a trashcan icon then you might remove it from the DOM.

If you want some browser independence and more sophistication then you can use the jQuery UI draggable and droppable widgets. Using these is easy, but there are a lot of options and methods, not to mention css stylings you can make use of. The simplest example is just to drag a button.

First we need to load jQuery and the latest version of jQuery UI:

```
<link rel="stylesheet" href="//code.jquery.com/ui/1.12.1/themes/
                                    smoothness/jquery-ui.css">
<script
  src="https://code.jquery.com/jquery-3.1.1.js"
  integrity=  "sha256-16cdPddA6VdVInumRGo6IbivbERE8p7CQR3HzTBuELA="
  crossorigin="anonymous">
</script>
<script src="//code.jquery.com/ui/1.12.1/jquery-ui.js"></script>
```

Assuming we have the same button defined in HTML we can make it draggable using:

```
$("#button1").draggable({ cancel:false });
```

After this the user can drag the button and drop it anywhere on the page. The option cancel:false isn't usually needed, but it is for a button because the click event occurs before the drag can begin.

You can also make any object the target of a drop using the droppable widget. In this case using it is slightly more difficult in that you have to provide at least an event handler for the drop event.

For example, if you add another element to the page with id dropTarget then you can handle a drop onto it using:

```
$("#dropTarget").droppable({
                     drop: function() {
                          alert("dropped");
                     }
             });
```

Now when the button is dropped on it you will see the alert box. There are lots of options and methods that help you control and customize the drag and drop in jQuery UI but this is the basic mechanism.

Finally we have HTML5 drag and drop. Making something draggable is just a matter of setting the draggable attribute to true:

```
$("#button1").prop("draggable", "true");
```

After this the button will be draggable but when the user drops it the result is that it returns to its original position. To make something happen you have to handle the drop event and often one or more of:

- dragstart
- drag
- dragenter
- dragleave
- dragover
- dragend

Not every type of element can be made the target of a drop. For example, to handle the drop of the button onto the document surface we would need to define the drop event and override the dragover and dragenter events to stop the default behavior:

```
$(document).on("drop",
             function(event){
                 event.preventDefault();
                 alert("drop");
             })
       .on("dragover",
             function(event){
                 event.preventDefault();
             })
       .on("dragenter",
             function (event) {
                 event.preventDefault();
             });
```

With these functions defined you can drag and drop the button and produce the alert.

If you want to actually move the button to its new location then you have to use some complicated techniques. The idea is that with every drag and drop there is some data that is being transferred and this is done using the dataTransfer object. This has set and get methods that allow you to store and retrieve MIME formatted data. For example, to pass the id of the object being dragged you would use:

```
event.originalEvent.dataTransfer
                   .setData("text/plain", event.target.id);
```

You can arrange for a range of different data types to be dragged and when the drop event occurs the data can be retrieved using getData.

A complete drag and drop event handler set is:

```
$("#button1").css("position", "absolute");
$("#button1").prop("draggable", "true");

$(document)
  .on("dragstart",
        function (event) {
           event.originalEvent.dataTransfer
               .setData("text/plain", event.target.id);
        })
    .on("drop",
           function (event) {
              event.preventDefault();
              var id = event.originalEvent.dataTransfer
                                          .getData("text");
              $("#" + id).css("top", event.pageY)
                         .css("left", event.pageX);
           })
    .on("dragover",
           function (event) {
              event.preventDefault();
           })
    .on("dragenter",
           function (event) {
              event.preventDefault();
           });
```

If you try this out then you will be able to drag the button to a new location and drop it there.

In general HTML5 drag and drop is much more designed to allow you to drag data from one element to another. There are lots of other facilities including the ability to specify a drag icon and customize the behavior in other ways.

So which should you use?

If you already use the jQuery UI then using its draggable and droppable widgets is probably the best way to go. Without the jQuery UI then it might seem that the best solution is to use HTML5, however, there are many differences in the way that browsers have implemented the standard. As time goes on things are getting better, but there is still a place for the direct JavaScript approach to drag and drop using mousedown, mousemove and mouseup.

## Keyboard Events

There are three keyboard events:

- keypress
- keydown
- keyup

We need to look first at keypress.

### keypress

keypress is fired when a single key press has been completed and there is a character ready to be processed. Keys that do not create an input character such as Shift do not fire the keypress event. Only the element that has the current focus will receive keypress events. If you want to handle all of the keyboard input on a page attach the event handler to document.

For example:

```
$(document).keypress(
            function(event){
              console.log(event.which);
            });
```

The code that which is set to is a character code that corresponds to the character the key produces. That is, the code that you get from a particular key depends on how the operating system has configured the keyboard i.e. it depends on the language the keyboard supports. The which property is set to a 16 bit value that corresponds to the UTF-16 code for a character in Plane 0, the Basic Multilingual Plane (BMP). This corresponds to the 65,536 characters that you can type on a keyboard by selecting an appropriate language. There are a few lists of symbols in the BMP but the Unicode list is presumably authoritative http://unicode.org/roadmaps/bmp/.

If you would like to convert the UTF-16 code to a string all you need is fromCharCode:

```
$(document).keypress(
            function(event){
              console.log(event.which);
              console.log(String.fromCharCode(event.which));
            });
```

To see this in action try installing some different country keyboards and try typing the same key with each one selected. In many cases the keycode and character displayed will be different. See Chapter 14 for more information on Unicode and encodings.

### keydown and keyup

The most important thing to realize is that keydown and keyup are different from keypress. These two events work with the keys and not the character that the key produces. The keydown event is fired when the user presses any key down including the non-printing or silent keys such as shift and the cursor keys. The keyup event is fired when a key is released. If the operating system auto repeats the key then the keydown and keyup event are fired for each repeat.

The which property of the event object returns the key code of the key involved in the event. This doesn't change no matter what symbol the key actually produces. The key codes assigned to the keys corresponding to printable characters are generally the UTF-16 code for the character. For example, the A key on the standard PC keyboard returns keycode 65 which is the UTF-16 (and ASCII) code for "A". However, this is the code that is returned if you press the shift key at the same time or not, or if you configure the keyboard to return some other character.

```
$(document).keydown(
            function(event){
              console.log(event.which);
              console.log(String.fromCharCode(event.which));
            });
```

There are lists of key codes and most are standard but you need to realize the range of keys available depends on the device the keyboard is designed to work with. You really should only make use of the most common keys.

Typically keydown and keyup are used to provide instant input to games. For example the arrow or cursor keys can be used to "steer" a sprite: in this case up is 38, right is 39, left is 37 and down is 40.

# Form Events

Forms are a very standard way of getting input from the user and as such are the next obvious thing to consider after mouse and keyboard events.

There are a set of events associated with the movement of the focus from one element to another. The element that has the focus is the one that user input is directed at, and this is what makes it important.

### focus and blur

The focus event fires when an element gets the focus and the blur event fires when it loses it. In modern browsers any element can fire the focus and blur events even if it isn't within a form element. These events don't bubble up to parents.

### focusin and focusout

These are bubbling versions of focus and blur. That is, an element will receive this event if any of its children gets or loses the focus.

There are two events associated with detecting when the user has changed data in a form:

### change

The change event is fired when the value of an input, textarea or select element changes. For checkboxes and radio buttons the event is fired at once so that you can process the user's new selection. For input and textarea the event is only fired after the element loses focus. The reason for this is that the user may well be editing and changing what they are entering, and rather than fire a change event for each keystroke, the system waits until the user moves to another field in the form before informing you of the change.

### select

Now we come to a difficult event because what you do after it generally depends on the browser. The select event is triggered when the user selects some text by dragging in either an input text field or a textarea box. This much is easy but usually after this you need to access the selection and this used to be very browser specific. Unfortunately jQuery doesn't normalize this but there are jQuery plugins that do. Modern browsers that support HTML5, however, do provide a standard way to work with selected text. The input text and textarea elements support the selectionStart and selectionEnd attributes and these are easy to access using the jQuery prop function. The attributes give the start and end position of the selection in the String returned by the val function.

For example, if we have the following textarea:

```
<textarea id="edit">text</textarea>
```

Then we can work with the selection using an event handler:

```
$("#edit").select(
            function(event){
               var edit= $(event.target);
               var start= edit.prop("selectionStart");
               var end=edit.prop("selectionEnd");
               var text=edit.val();
               text=text.slice(start,end);
               edit.val(text);
            });
```

The event.target is wrapped as a jQuery object and then the prop func is used to retrieve the start and end of the selection. The contents of the textarea are then retrieved using val. The start and end are then used to reduce the string to just the selection and this is made the new contents of the textarea. The result is that only the characters that are selected remain in the textarea.

This is typical of how text manipulation works. The markers, start and end, are retrieved and used to process the contents of the text field as a string which is restored to make the changes visible to the user.

### submit

The final form event is submit. This is fired when the user submits the form. Generally you use an event handler to make any final validation needed but always remember that validation is best performed early if at all possible. It is also used to fire the submit action on the form so that you can use elements other than a submit button.

For more information and examples see the Forms chapter in the companion volume *Just jQuery: The Core UI*.

## Browser Events

There are only two browser generated events that jQuery specifically handles related to the viewing window – size and scrolling elements.

### resize

The resize event is fired whenever the user resizes the browser window. Obviously the purpose of this event is to give you the opportunity to modify the layout or sometimes to restrict the size change. The only real problem with handling resize is that different browsers fire the event in different ways. Some fire the event every time the user adjusts the size of the window and others only fire it once at the end of the resize. Sometimes this doesn't cause any difficulty because the resize handler doesn't do very much work. However, in many cases the resize event handler has a lot of work to do and it slows the UI down too much. The good news is that all modern browsers – Firefox, Chrome, IE 11 and Edge - fire the event only when the user drops the window border.

### scroll

This event is fired on any element that has an overflow property set to scroll or auto when scroll is being used. It fires no matter how the scroll has occurred – via mouse or keyboard. In most cases you can allow the browser to take care of the scroll implementation but sometimes you need to intervene.

For example if you want to generate content as the user scrolls an element:

```
<div id="target"
     style="overflow: scroll; width: 200px; height: 100px;">
#</br>
#</br>
#</br>
#</br>
#</br>
</div>
```

This starts off with just a column of hashes. When the user scrolls to see more content the scroll event is triggered and the event handler called:

```
var count=0;
$("#target").scroll(
                function() {
                  count++;
                  $( "#target" ).append(count.toString()+ "</br>" );
                });
```

In this case we simply append the value of a counter.

A common occurrence is the use of the jQuery scrollleft and scrolltop functions within scroll event handlers to discover how far the element has been scrolled and to test for a horizontal or vertical scroll. You can also use them to set the scroll position. The positions are returned in pixels that are currently scrolled off the left or top.

## Document Events

The only important document event provided by jQuery is ready. This is fired when the DOM is fully loaded. However, this is not as simple as it might sound. You want to run your JavaScript when the resources that it works with are ready, but there is no simple definition of when a page is "ready". The fact that your JavaScript is about to modify the page indicates that there is a sense in which the page still isn't "ready".

There is also the matter of where you start your JavaScript loading. Unless you use the async or defer attributes a script is loaded and the processing of the page stops until it has been executed and releases the UI thread. That is, script loading is by default synchronous with the processing of the page.

If you place your script tag in the head section then the browser will stop rendering the page and download your code. In this case you need to use the ready event to make sure that the DOM is ready for you to work with it.

However, if you place the script tag at the end of the page the browser will download your code and run it after showing the user the page. This can make it look as if your page loads faster.

There is also the complication of the async and defer attributes. If you use async then the script is loaded in the background and executes as soon as it is ready. If you use defer then the script is loaded asynchronously but not executed until the page is parsed.

It is generally held that you get the best perceived load time by placing any JavaScript loads at the very end of the page. However, if you do this you cannot have any code higher up the page that makes use of the code loaded at the end. You also don't need to use the jQuery ready event as the page will be loaded and ready before your code is loaded and ready. One disadvantage is that the user could start to interact with the page before your code is usable.

Another problem is that you have to make sure that jQuery is loaded before your code tries to make use of it. You can't even make use of the ready event if jQuery isn't loaded. This may seem obvious but it is a common error.

If you want to be safe, load jQuery in the header without specifying async or defer. Then place your code in a ready event handler anywhere on the page below the loading of jQuery. You can include an async or defer attribute on your own code if you want to avoid blocking the UI.

You can use the ready event in a number of ways but the preferred method is:

```
$(handler);
```

A typical way to work with jQuery is:

```
<head>
 <title>TODO supply a title</title>
 <meta charset="UTF-8">
 <meta name="viewport" content="width=device-width,
                                initial-scale=1.0">
 <script
   src="https://code.jquery.com/jquery-3.1.1.js"
   integrity="sha256-16cdPddA6VdVInumRGo6IbivbERE8p7CQR3HzTBuELA="
   crossorigin="anonymous">
 </script>
 <script>
  $(function () {
     your code
     });
 </script>
</head>
```

Notice that placing your code inside a ready event handler has the beneficial side-effect of making all of the variables you create local variables which are accessible only from your code. This is another example of closure working in our favor.

It is worth mentioning that the ready event makes use of the jQuery.ready function which returns a Promise object. Promises and deferreds are discussed in Chapter 4, but you could write in place of $(handler):

```
$.when($.ready).then(handler);
```

There is no particular advantage to this. There might be an advantage if you need to compose promises to make more complicated behavior. You can also use it for error handling. More on these topics in Chapters 4 and 5.

## Events and More Events

In this chapter we have covered the events that jQuery deems important enough to have their own functions. This is a relatively small set of the events that a typical browser supports. For example, the MDN Event Reference has a very long list of standard events and an equally long list of non-standard events.

You can use any of these events via jQuery using the on, one and off functions to attach handlers. You might think that you are safe to use the standard events but all you can assume is a reasonable expectation that modern browsers will have implemented them. What you cannot assume is that they have implemented them in the same way. Small differences in implementation often cause big problems, and unfortunately jQuery offers no help in smoothing over browser differences for the vast majority of events.

For example, the wheel event is the standard for detecting when a mouse wheel has been rotated. You can use it something like:

```
$(document).on("wheel",
               function(event){
                  console.log(event.originalEvent.deltaY);
               });
```

Notice that to access the deltaY property we need to use the originalEvent object because jQuery doesn't unpack this into its event object. The deltaY is negative and positive according to which way the wheel has been rotated.

This is easy,but until recently the wheel event didn't work with Safari or with Edge. Finding out which browsers support which events isn't easy and finding out exactly how they support them is even harder. In practice all you can reasonably do is to try your program out on the browsers that you need to support.

## Immediate Events

So far the key idea in understanding JavaScript and event handling has been the idea that JavaScript has only one thread of execution (unless you create others using web workers say). What this means for events is that only one event handler can be active at any given moment. If another event occurs while an event handler or any JavaScript is running then, it is simply added to the event queue and it gets its chance to run when the currently executing code stops running and frees the thread. This is sometimes explained as "run to completion" in the sense that any JavaScript that is running runs until it is completed and isn't interrupted by the system to do something else.

This really is the big idea but like all principles there are minor exceptions and these aren't well documented or particularly well thought out.

Consider for a moment the following program:

```
$("#button1").click(
            function(){
              $("#button2").click();
              console.log("button click 1");
            });

$("#button2").click(
            function(){
              console.log("button click 2");
            });
```

Two buttons each with their own click event handlers that display messages on the console. The complication  is that the first button click handler fires the click event on the second button.

What do you see on the console log?

By the "run to completion" rule the first button's event handler should fire the click event on button2, which should be added to the event queue to all the currently executing event handlers to complete. So you should see button click 1 followed by button click 2.

You don't – you actually see button click 2 followed by button click 1.

When you fire an event in code it behaves more like a function call. Indeed this is exactly what is happening when you fire an event in software, all that happens is that the functions that are stored in the list of event handlers are called one after another. There is still only a single thread of execution but it transfers to the other event handler before completing the current event handler.

This is something we will have to return to when we look at custom events in the next chapter.

There are also examples where an event handler is called immediately when a real not a just a software event occurs but these are rare, very browser and even OS dependent. The one that is usually quoted is the firing of a resize event while an Alert is shown on the screen.

The important point is that JavaScript is single-threaded and only one thing happens at a time, but the rules for how control is passed from one event handler to another can be more complicated than you might expect.

# Summary

- There are five categories of event that jQuery provides special shortcut functions for: mouse, keyboard, form, browser and document.

- Mouse events are most familiar. The click event is safe to use with touch screen devices as it is generally fired if the user taps. The double click event is best avoided. The right click is handled using the context menu event and this generally works on touch devices as a long tap.

- The lower level mouse events – mousedown, mouseup and mousemove are best avoided for touch devices.

- Click works only with the prime button, usually the left button. You can program your own click event for the other buttons using mousedown and mouseup.

- Mousemove can be used to provide the user with free-form interaction, but any handler has to be short to avoid blocking the UI.

- A drag and drop operation needs the coordinated use of mousedown, mousemove and mouse up. It is easy to implement from first principles, but you could also use jQuery UI or the HTML5 drag and drop.

- Keyboard events respond either to the particular key that has been pressed or the character that the key generates.

- The keypress event is fired when a complete keypress has occurred and it returns the actual character the key generates taking account of any other keys pressed at the time. The keydown and keyup events fire on a key being pressed down or released respectively and they return a keycode which identifies the key, not the character it generates.

- Form events are concerned with detecting when form elements gain or lose focus and with changes the user makes to the data they hold.

- Browser events are concerned with letting you know when the UI needs to take account of changes in the display. The resize event if fired when the browser window is resized so you can re-arrange elements.

- The scroll event is fired when the document or a scrollable element has been scrolled.

- The only document event is ready which is fired when the DOM is built and ready to work with. How to load scripts and when to run them is a complex issue but the simplest thing to do is load jQuery in the head section and either use the ready event to run your program or place your program at the end of the page.

- There are lots of other events that you can use with the help of jQuery but as soon as you stray from the most used there is the problem of browser support and browser variations.

- If you fire an event in software, it isn't run asynchronously. It is an example of an immediate event and it is more like a function call to the list of event handlers.

# Chapter 4

# Asynchronous Code

Events are central to the programming in JavaScript and most programmers master their use early on. Asynchronous programming is just another aspect of an event driven environment, but this is much more difficult to master. Let's find out what the relationship is and why it is so difficult.

**A JavaScript program is a collection of event handlers waiting for something to happen.**

When something does happen the event causes the attached event handlers to run. Once we are into the event handler this is just standard programming, nothing new here, but for a single threaded language like JavaScript this isn't quite true. As we have already discussed in the previous chapter, the thread of execution that does the work in an event handler is also the thread that responds to the user interface UI. If an event handler takes too long then the UI freezes.

So how can an event handler that cannot avoid doing something that takes a long time keep the UI responsive?

First notice that an event handler can initiate processes that take an incredibly long time compared to the speed that a JavaScript program runs. For example if you use AJAX to download a file or do anything connected with the network then the time to complete the action is likely to be seconds and perhaps minutes. If the event handler waits for the task to complete then the UI freezes for a very unacceptable time.

Using a single threaded event based UI forces us to introduce the idea of asynchronous tasks or functions.

Ordinarily a function will return when it has finished running its code. This is generally called a synchronous or blocking function because it blocks the UI thread until it is complete. To avoid blocking the UI thread we need to invent non-blocking functions that return as soon as possible and nearly always before they have completed their task.

A non-blocking function sets a process in motion and then returns to the calling program.

This allows the calling program to do whatever it has to and then return to allow the thread to process the UI.

This all seems very nice but you can see that there is a problem and it is a big problem.

The non-blocking function returns before it has completed and this means that the event handler returns before it has the result of the call, so the job isn't done. We need to activate some code to process the results of the non-blocking function.

How are we to do this?

The standard solution is to provide a callback function to the non-blocking function. A callback is a function that the non-blocking process calls when it has really finished its task.

As functions are first class objects in JavaScript using callbacks is relatively easy – you don't have to invent extra ideas such as delegates (C#), anonymous classes (Java) and lambdas (almost all languages) - to pass a function as a parameter. In fact you almost certainly have been using callbacks for a long time perhaps without realizing their connection to events.

A callback is like an event handler which fires when the non-blocking function complete its task.

You can even implement a callback so that it looks exactly like an event.

For example, consider the AJAX get function, more about which in later chapters, which simply downloads the specified file from the server:

```
$.get("test.txt",function(data){ alert(data); });
```

In this case the callback is an anonymous function that simply displays the data stored in the file. Notice that if the get was a blocking function the code would read:

```
$.get("test.txt");
alert(data);
```

and there would be no need for a function of any sort.

It is easy, but a little messy, to convert this to an event on an object. To do this we need an object with a new get function that will download the specified URL and then raise the loaded event:

```
var ajax=$({});

ajax.get=function(url){
        $.get(url,
            function(data){
                trigger("loaded",data);
            });
        };
```

Notice that now the callback function simply fires the loaded event with data as the custom data object.

To use this new get method on the new AJAX object all we have to do is register an event handler and call the method:

```
ajax.on("loaded",
        function(data){
          alert(data);
        });
ajax.get("test.txt");
```

Now when the file has downloaded the loaded event is fired on the AJAX object and the event handler is called.

You can see that it is a matter of taste whether you use a callback or an event for the completion of a non-blocking function. In practice the DOM makes use of events and JavaScript makes use of callbacks, but this isn't a hard and fast rule. If an object is involved, events are also more natural.

## The Problem With Asynchronous

Callbacks may be like event handlers, but they way that they occur in code makes them a very different proposition. Event handlers are in the main easy to write and cause few problems, but callbacks have some serious problems. The reason for this difference is that event handlers are set up by code that has no interest in their results. When you set a button's click handler the code that sets it generally doesn't want to interact with the click handler later in time when a click occurs. It's a set and forget operation. In other words, event handlers are usually fairly closed pieces of code that don't depend on anything else.

Callbacks, on the other hand, generally do something that the code that sets them up cares about. Generally you want to download a file and process the data it contains. In an ideal world the download would complete and then the code would continue on its way to process the file. When you have to use a callback this isn't the way it happens – the process is initiated and the code that started it comes to an end; only later does the callback activate and the process is completed elsewhere.

This is more difficult.

You will hear lots of explanations of the problem of asynchronous code along the lines of "callback hell", and the "callback pyramid of doom". These are problems but they arise from taking particular approaches to asynchronous programming.

The first problem is that raw asynchronous programming distorts the intended flow of control.

In a synchronous program you might write

```
loadA();
loadB();
loadC();
```

and you can expect A to load before B which loads before C.

As soon as you convert these to async operations you can't be sure what order things are done in unless you adopt the callback cascade:

```
loadA(loadB(loadC()));
```

where each function accepts a callback as its parameter.

The callback approach to async turns sequential default flow of control into nested function calls. But keep in mind that the callback approach is just one of many. Because it is so widely used, there is a tendency to think that a callback is the only way to deal with asynchronous code.

## Asynchronous Flow Of Control and Closure

The effect that asynchronous code has on the structure of your program is easy to understand in terms of what code goes before and what code goes after:

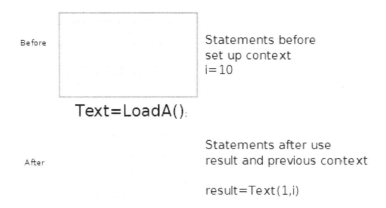

The statements that are before the asynchronous operation provide the context for the call. Variables which are set in this before code may contain values that are important for what to do with the result of the asynchronous operation in the code to follow it. The code that follows it makes use of the result of the operation and the context established by the earlier code.

When you use a callback the code that follows the call to the asynchronous function doesn't follow – it becomes another function.

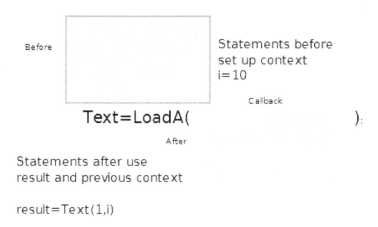

Before

Statements before
set up context
i=10

Callback

**Text=LoadA(** ):

After

Statements after use
result and previous context

result=Text(1,i)

That is, the "after" code – becomes the callback:

You can now see that the flow of control has been distorted – what was one function is now two. Don't worry too much about it at the moment but this isn't a complete picture of what can happen because if the Callback contains an asynchronous call you repeat the procedure of moving the "after" code into a callback – distorting the flow of control again.

Not only that but in a simple programming environment the context is lost. As the "after" code is now a separate function it no longer has access to the variables contained in the "before" code. In short, the callback can't perform an instruction like Text(1,i) because i isn't only out of scope it doesn't even exist.

Except of course in JavaScript it does.

JavaScript supports closure and this means that the variables that were in scope when a function was created remain in scope for it even if from the point of view of other parts of the program they have long been destroyed. That means the callback does have access to the variable i and can perform result=Text(1,i) because closure provides all of the variables that were defined when it was.

There are many complex and esoteric explanations of what closure is and why you might want it, but it is this automatic provision of context to a callback function that seems the most convincing. There are lots of other uses of closure, but it is this one that you would invent closure for.

**Closures ensure that callbacks have their context.**

Of course things can be more complicated. It could be that the asynchronous function call is itself nested within a control structure that spans the before and after block of code.

For example, if a callback is in a for loop then the loop executes and completes, possibly before any of the callbacks are activated. Similarly, an if statement cannot test the result of a callback because this isn't available at the time the code is executed. Closures solve many of the problems of callbacks, but not all.

## Asynchronous Errors

It is clear that using callbacks makes a mess of the flow of control of a program and it is difficult to ensure that everything happens in the correct order. However, often the order in which callbacks occur isn't important. For example, if you are loading a set of files it usually doesn't matter what order they are loaded in as long they do load and are processed. A more common problem, and one that is often ignored, is what should happen when an error occurs. It has to be admitted that this is often a problem in synchronous code as well.

The big difference in asynchronous code is that the error problem can occur at any time after the callbacks have been set and in any order. In a synchronous blocking program you might write:

```
try{
 load A
 load B
 load C
}
catch(e){
 deal with a problem
}
```

If you change the load functions to asynchronous functions then the catch doesn't catch any of the errors that the loads might produce and certainly not any that the callbacks might create. The reason is simply that the catch clause is executed before any of this code actually runs and it is well in the past when any errors might actually occur.

Handling errors is a big problem for asynchronous programs because it is difficult to know the state of the system when the error occurs. If file B fails to download what to do might depend on whether file A or C downloaded or not. The simplest way of dealing with errors is to provide an alternative callback that is used if the asynchronous function fails. For example:

```
load(A,success,error)
```

where success is called if the load works and error is called otherwise

Error handling is one of the big advantages of using Promises to wrap callbacks – more of this in Chapters 4 and 5.

## The Callbacks List

There is an internal facility that jQuery uses to implement various callback related features. The Callbacks object can be used to keep a list of callbacks and trigger them all with a single command. This isn't often useful but if you plan to implement callback features in your own components then it can simplify things.

The function:

```
var callback=$.CallBacks(options);
```

returns a callbacks list object. Once you have a callbacks list object you can use the add method to add functions and the remove method to remove functions from the list. To execute the callback list  all you have to do is use the fire method. There is also the disable method that stops the callbacks being fired while keeping the list intact. If you use an array of functions then you can add and remove a set of callbacks in one go.

The options are a space separated list of strings consisting of:

- once: Ensures the callback list can only be fired once
- memory: Keeps track of previous values and will call any callback added after the list has been fired as it is added
- unique: Ensures a callback can only be added once
- stopOnFalse: Interrupts callings when a callback returns false.

Using these and some other functions you can equip an object with a callback list and control exactly how it can be fired.

## The Function Queue – Sequential Async

Surprisingly one of the most commonly encountered problems is how to make async functions run in a particular order. If you make three async calls:

```
functionA();
functionB();
functionC();
```

then as already explained the problem is that A returns before it is complete and B is started almost at once followed by C. You can't say what order they will complete in and effectively they are running at the same time.

If you want the advantage of an async function, i.e. keeping the UI responsive, but still want the functions to execute in a fixed order, you have a problem. If each of the functions accepts a callback that is triggered when it finishes then you can write a sequential flow of control as:

```
functionA(functionB(functionC));
```

but this is often not possible and when it is the resulting code looks confusing.

A better solution is to use a function queue and jQuery provides this facility because it needs it to choreograph its animation functions which are all asynchronous. The function queue was described in detail and with respect to its use in animation in *Just jQuery: The Core UI* but as it is a key idea in asynchronous functions it is covered here more quickly and more generally.

Every element can have any number of function queues associated with it. Essentially a function queue is just an array used to store functions. To create a queue you can make use of the .queue function.

For example, to add a function to the function queue of all divs you would use something like:

```
$("div").queue("myQueue",myFunction);
```

You can also set up a queue on an empty object if you don't want to associate it with a particular element or object:

```
var obj=$({}).queue("myQueue",myF1)
             .queue("myQueue",myF2)
             .queue("myQueue",myF3)
```

After this the queue has three functions stored in it.

There are some functions to access and manipulate the queue:

| | |
|---|---|
| .queue("queueName") | returns the queue as an array |
| .queue("queueName",newQueue) | replaces the queue with the array of functions specified by newQueue |
| .clearQueue("queueName") | removes all the functions in the queue. |

The whole point of a function queue is to dequeue functions from it when you need to execute them.

For example, with the three-function queue associated with obj in the previous example:

```
obj.dequeue("myQueue");
```

will result in myF1 being executed. That is all that happens – dequeue runs a single function. If you want to execute the next function you need to use dequeue again:

```
obj.dequeue("myQueue");
```

runs myF2.

This doesn't seem particularly useful until you realize that you can put the dequeue in the functions that are in the queue. In this way you can build up a queue and include in each of the functions a dequeue command when it is time for the next function to run. Notice this works for async and synchronous functions. It is such a common way to use a queue that since jQuery 1.4 the function queue has passed the next function in the queue as the first argument to the function currently being dequeued. This makes it possible to call the next function and dequeue it without having to keep a reference to the object that the queue is hosted by.

What this means is that any function in the queue can start the next function by simply using

```
next();
```

where next is the first argument passed to the function.

The best way to see how all this works is to look at a general asynchronous call. For example, the AJAX get example we looked at earlier. If you want to load two files then the simplest thing to do is:

```
$.get("test.txt",function(data){ console.log(data);});
$.get("test_1.txt",function(data){ console.log(data);});
```

However, you cannot know which file will load first. If you want to always load test and then load test_1 you would have to write something like:

```
$.get("test.txt",
        function (data) {
           console.log(data);
           $.get("test_1.txt",
                   function (data) {
                      console.log(data);
                   });
        });
```

You can see that the second get is only performed when the first get's callback is activated. It isn't difficult to follow this with just two files, but it gets increasingly difficult with more files. This is the origin of "callback hell" as the indentation needed to keep track of callbacks within callbacks increases and increases.

One solution is to use the function queue. To do this we first need to wrap the functions we want to call and add a call to next at the point we want the next function to start work:

```
var getQ1 = function (next) {
          $.get("test.txt",
                  function (data) {
                    console.log(data);
                    next();
                  });
        };
```

We also need to wrap the second asynchronous function in the same way:

```
var getQ2 = function (next) {
          $.get("test_1.txt",
                  function (data) {
          console.log(data);
          next();
        });
      };
```

Now all we have to do is add them to a queue and start things running:

```
var q = $({}).queue("myQ",getQ1);
q.queue("myQ",getQ2);
q.dequeue("myQ");
```

Now the second file will not start loading until the first has been loaded and processed.

The same sort of approach solves most of the problems of running asynchronous functions sequentially. Notice that the call to next() doesn't have to occur at the very end of the asynchronous function. It can be placed anywhere it is allowable to start the next function in the queue so there can be an overlap.

The big problem is handling any errors that might occur. The most direct approach is to have each of the functions check for an error and then do something appropriate like trying the action again or simply clearing the queue:

```
if(error) q.clearQueue("myQ");
```

Notice that in this simple form the functions in the queue have to have access to the object on which the queue is defined and the name of the queue. In this case q is a global variable and the queue name was set earlier.

If you want to restart the entire queue a given number of times then you need to make sure that there is a copy that can be started when an error occurs.

## Queue Functions With Parameters

A particular problem with the function queue is that it cannot be used with functions that require parameters. Some go to the trouble of implementing their own function queue complete with parameters or augmenting the function queue with a separate parameter queue. This isn't necessary because we can use closure to replace parameter passing. This is a general pattern that can be used whenever you need to pass parameters to a function, but cannot use parameters.

For example, suppose we want to pass the file name to the AJAX file download function. This can be done by creating a function that creates the function we want to add to the function queue – that is we need to use an object factory. The reason is simply that any variables that are in scope when the object factory creates the function will be accessible from that function:

```
var GETQ = function (file) {
            var f = function (next) {
             $.get(file,
         function (data) {
           console.log(data);
           next();
         });
        };
    return f;
    };
```

Now GETQ is not the function we are placing in the queue, instead it returns the function that we are placing in the queue. Also, notice that the parameters of GETQ are in scope when the function f is created, and so they can all be used by it courtesy of closure.

Now to add the function to the queue we have to call GETQ with the parameters we want to use:

```
var q = $({}).queue("myQ",GETQ("test.txt"));
q.queue("myQ",GETQ("test_1.txt"));
q.dequeue("myQ");
```

Notice that we actually have to call the function so that it creates the function that is placed in the queue.

This is a general pattern that you can use to pass parameters and additional parameters to any function. Simply write an object factory that accepts the parameters and creates the function. The parameters are made available to the created function by the operation of closure.

## Custom Asynchronous Functions

Asynchronous functions in JavaScript mainly relate to file transfer and animation. However, you can implement your own asynchronous functions to avoid blocking the UI thread. Key to doing this are the setInterval and setTimeOut functions. These will place a message in the event queue that calls a function after a set time. The setInterval function arranges to call the function repeatedly at the set interval.

You may already be familiar with these functions as ways of calling functions after a delay or regularly, but they can also be used to create a custom asynchronous function. All you have to do is call setTimeOut with a delay of zero:

```
setTimeout(function(){do something},0);
```

This effectively puts the function on the event queue and then returns immediately. Of course, the function will not be processed by the event queue until the UI thread is released.

A simple example should make this clear:

```
console.log("before");
setTimeout(function () {
            console.log("MyAsyncFunction");
                  }, 0);
console.log("after");
```

The sequence of events is that first "before" is sent to the log, then the function is added to the event queue with a timeout of 0, but the function cannot be called until the UI thread is freed. The setTimeout returns at once and "after" is sent to the log and the UI thread is freed, assuming this is the last JavaScript instruction. Only then does the function get to run and send "MyAsyncFunction" to the log.

You can see that the order of execution is not what you might expect and this is asynchronous behavior. Notice also that the event queue is processed in whatever order the events occurred in, and if there is an event waiting to be processed it could be done before your custom function is called. You can make use of this to break up a long running function so as to keep the UI responsive.

The general idea is very simple, but the details vary according to the algorithm. As a simple example, suppose you want to compute pi to a few digits using the series:

```
pi=4*(1-1/3+1/5-1/7 ... and so on)
```

This is very easy to implement but to get pi to a reasonable number of digits you have to compute a lot of terms.

The simple-minded synchronous approach is to write something like:

```
$("#go").click(computePi);
function computePi() {
 var pi = 0;
 var k;
 for (k = 1; k <= 100000; k++) {
  pi += 4 * Math.pow(-1, k + 1) / (2 * k - 1);
  $("#result").text(pi);
  $("#count").text(k);
 }
}
```

where the DOM elements are provided by:

```
<div id="result">
0
</div>
<div id="count">
0
</div>
<button id="go">Go</button>
```

The intention is to display the progress of the calculation by changing the text displayed in the two divs each time through the for loop. If you try it out what you will find is that the UI freezes for some minutes and nothing is displayed in the web page until the loop finishes and the UI thread is freed to tend to the UI.

To keep the UI responsive, and in this case to see the intermediate results, we have to turn the calculation into an asynchronous function using setTimeout. We do this by breaking the calculation in small chunks – say 1000 iterations each. To do this we need a state object that records the state of the calculation so that it can be resumed:

```
var state = {};
state.k = 0;
state.pi = 0;
```

The function now performs 1000 iterations and then updates the text in the divs.

To enable the UI to stay responsive, the function then terminates but not before setting itself up in the event queue ready to perform another 1000 iterations after the UI has been updated:

```
function computePi() {
 if (state.k >= 100000000) return;
 var i;
 for (i = 0; i < 1000; i++) {
  state.k++;
  state.pi += 4 * Math.pow(-1, state.k + 1) / (2 * state.k - 1);
 }
 $("#result").text(state.pi);
 $("#count").text(state.k);
 setTimeout(computePi, 0);
}
```

If you run this version of the computation you will find that not only does the UI remain responsive you get to see the intermediate values as the calculation proceeds. Notice that the computePi function is now almost asynchronous in that it returns after doing 1000 iterations. You can change it to be truly async by, for example, using a function to setTimeout for the first call and return.

That is:

```
function computePiAsync(){
   setTimeout(computePi, 0);
}
```

Notice also that the function is able to access the state object because it is a global variable. If you don't want to use a global variable then create the computePi function inside another function and rely on closure to make the state variable accessible e.g.

```
function computePiAsync(){
 var state = {};
 state.k = 0;
 state.pi = 0;
 function computePi() {
  if (state.k >= 100000000) return;
  var i;
  for (i = 0; i < 1000; i++) {
   state.k++;
   state.pi +=4 * Math.pow(-1, state.k + 1) / (2 * state.k - 1);
  }
  $("#result").text(state.pi);
  $("#count").text(state.k);
  setTimeout(computePi, 0);
 }
 setTimeout(computePi, 0);
};
```

You can use the same technique to turn nearly any long running computation into an asynchronous procedure. All you have to do is break the computation down into small parts and preserve the state of the computation at the end of each chunk so that it can be restarted. Write the function so that it takes the state object and continues the computation. This is always possible, even if the task isn't to sum a mathematical series. For example, if you want to perform a complex database operation simply save the point in the transaction that you have reached.

There are some problems that you might encounter using setTimeout. The most common is that you do not get a zero timeout in practice. The obvious reason is that the function is not called until the code that used the setTimeout finishes. There also might be other events that need to be processed before the function is called. In addition different browsers set minimum times and 4ms is the shortest delay specified by HTML5. Often this makes no difference, but if you need the maximum efficiency then you need to take a different approach to implementing an asynchronous function, see Chapter 6.

You can also pass parameters to the delayed function but browsers differ in how they handle this. In most cases it is simpler to use closure to provide parameters. Also notice that when the function is called this will be the global window object, rather than what it was when you invoked setTimeout. This is generally only a problem if you try to call a function as an object method.

# Summary

- A JavaScript program is a collection of event handlers waiting for something to happen.

- There is only one thread of execution in a JavaScript program and if an event handler takes too long then the UI freezes.

- Using a single threaded event based UI forces us to introduce the idea of asynchronous tasks or functions that return before their work is complete – they are non-blocking.

- This in turn causes us to have to invent and use the idea of a callback function which is called to process the result of an asynchronous function.

- A callback is like an event handler that is fired when something happens in an asynchronous function.

- Callbacks, unlike events, distort the flow of control of your program and this makes error handling in particular more difficult.


- When using asynchronous functions closure is your friend. It keeps variables that were in scope when the function was created available to it and this provides a continuity of execution environment that makes it easier to continue the flow of control across the use of the callback.

- jQuery provides the callback object to manage lists of callbacks. This is mostly used in jQuery's re-implementation of the event system but you can make use of it within your own objects to maintain callback lists.

- jQuery's function queue gives you a way to ensure that asynchronous calls occur in a specified order.

- You can use closure to pass parameters to functions in the queue.

- Custom asynchronous functions can be created using setTimeout and these can be used, with the help of a state object, to break up a task and release the UI thread to keep the UI responsive.

# Chapter 5

## Consuming Promises

Promises are a way of organizing asynchronous calls that is better than using callbacks. The callbacks are still there but they come with a degree of organization. Previously jQuery was criticized for implementing a promise mechanism that was non-standard. Promises in jQuery 3 are compatible with the standard.

In this chapter we are going to look at using jQuery promises to create asynchronous code that is easy to understand and hard for bugs to hide in. Specifically we are going to look at how to use the promises that other functions return to use in place of callbacks. That is we are going to be looking at consuming promises.

In the next chapter we will look at how to add promise support to your own asynchronous code i.e. how to produce promises for others to use. This involves making use of another type of object – a Deferred which has all of the properties and methods of a promise and a few more.

## jQuery v JavaScript Promises

jQuery was a pioneer of promises and this was good but now means that its approach is slightly non-standard. It was very non-standard before jQuery 3, but now it works according to the standard with some extras and omissions.

Some people say that now promises are a part of JavaScript you should simply ignore jQuery's promise library. However, this isn't entirely possible if you want to make use of jQuery functions that return jQuery promises.

You can always convert a jQuery promise into a JavaScript promise using:

```
var JavaScript=Promise.resolve(jQueryPromise);
```

However, as in most cases in jQuery 3, as the jQuery Promise works in the same way as a JavaScript Promise there seems to be little reason to do this. My advice is to work with jQuery promises unless you really need to use some feature of a JavaScript promise that isn't available in jQuery.

At some point in the future it seems likely that jQuery will remove its version of promises and convert to using JavaScript promises and this should be possible without breaking your existing code.

In the rest of this chapter the focus will be on using jQuery promises and the few differences with JavaScript promises will be made clear. For most of the time you can forget that jQuery promises are anything different.

It is also worth mentioning that JavaScript standard promises are "thenables" which is essentially any object that has a then method. A thenable can be converted into a standard promise in the same way as a jQuery promise can be.

## What is the problem?

As should be perfectly clear by now the problem is that JavaScript is single-threaded and this means if you were to call any functions that need to wait while some external event occurs – a file to download say – then, for the duration of the event, your app would appear to freeze. The user interface, and events in particular, are all handled by the same thread and if that thread is in a wait state then nothing else gets done.

The usual solution to this problem as explained in earlier chapters is to use a callback function. The callback is passed to the function that is going to do the long job and instead of keeping the thread waiting it simply returns immediately. This allows the thread to do other work while it get on with its task. When it has finished it calls the callback function, usually with the result of the task. The callback function then processes the results.

Callbacks are difficult because they alter the flow of control in an unnatural way and this has been explained in an earlier chapter. However, it is worth saying that the precise problem that promises were introduced to solve is that of running asynchronous tasks one after the other. That is, if you have three asynchronous tasks and simply call them:

```
TaskA();
TaskB();
TaskC();
```

Then they will execute in an order that depends on how long each takes. They effectively run in parallel. If you want them to run sequentially – that is TaskB only starts after TaskA ends, and TaskC starts after TaskB ends, then you have to use some sort of mechanisms to signal the end of each task and initiate the next one in the sequence.

The callback solution is to use nested callbacks. Something like:

```
TaskA(callBackTaskB(callBackTaskC)));
```

where each task accepts a callback that is invoked when it ends. This looks simple enough in this example but this is because it is over simplified. In real life nested callbacks quickly degenerate into "callback hell" and there is no standard way of handling errors accept for having a success and a failure callback for each function.

Running sequential tasks is something promises make easy.

This is also the problem that jQuery's function queues solve and this is explained in Chapter 3. Promises are a more general approach to the whole problem of working with asynchronous functions and as such they are worth knowing about.

Let's look first at the basic operation of a Promise.

## The Basic Promise

An operation that takes some time will generally return a promise object at once and then complete its task in the background:

```
var mypromise=slowFun(args);
```

Notice that even though you get a promise object returned at once, it is unlikely that slowFun has finished whatever it is trying to do.

There is also the idea that the slow function is computing a value which your program is waiting for – this isn't necessarily the case as you could be just waiting for it to complete what it is doing. However, in most cases the promise is regarded as being a promise to deliver a future value and this view is often helpful.

**What do you do with a promise?**

The most common thing to do is to use its then method to set up what should happen when the slow function is complete:

```
mypromise.then(onComplete,onError,onProgress);
```

where onComplete is a function that is called when the slow function finishes its task. It is passed the value, or in jQuery's case a set of values, that the slow function generates on completion. That is, when the promise is fulfilled it supplies the value to the onComplete. The onError function is optional and is called if an error occurs while the slow function is executing. The value that the onError receives is the reason for the error. The onProgress function is called periodically to indicate progress – not all promise objects support this.

That is, you only have to specify the onComplete function if you don't want to handle the error or monitor progress, in which case onError and onProgress are optional.

A promise object is in one of three states.

- When it is first created it is **pending**.
- If the task ends correctly then it is in the **resolved** or **fulfilled** state.
- If the task ends with an error it enters the **rejected** state.

A promise is also said to be **settled** if it isn't pending i.e. if it is either fulfilled or rejected. Once a promise is settled its state and value doesn't change.

It is important to realize that there is no rush to use the then method, or any other method to define the functions to be called. The promise object's state determines if and when any of the functions are called. If a promise is already settled when you add functions as part of a then they will still be carried out. The key idea is that a promise always activates the onComplete, onError or onProgress after the code that is currently running has finished.

**That is a promise always executes its functions asynchronously.**

You can add as many onComplete, onError or onProgress functions as you want to. For example:

```
mypromise.then(onComplete1,onError1,onProgress1);
mypromise.then(onComplete2,onError2,onProgress2);
```

When the promise is settled, the handlers are called in the order that they were added.

## The AJAX Get With a Promise

An example of using a promise in a function that is potentially slow is provided by the jQuery AJAX get method, but in fact any of the AJAX functions work in the same sort of way.

The get method will return any file as specified by the URL you provide. Of course, it could take some time to return the file as it has to be downloaded. This is a perfect use of the promise object and the get method returns a promise.

So, for example, if you want to download the file you might use:

```
$.get("TextFile.txt");
```

which would start the file downloading using another thread of execution and return immediately.

How do you get the contents of the file when the task completes?

The early versions of jQuery didn't use promises and you had to supply callback functions within the get method. Since jQuery 1.5 all of the AJAX functions have returned a promise object, which is much easier to use.

To download a file you now simply have to keep a reference to the returned promise object:

```
var myPromise = $.get("TextFile.txt");
```

and make use of its then method to process the returned data:

```
myPromise.then(function (value) {
              console.log(value);
          });
```

You could also define functions to handle an error or report the progress of the download. In this case the anonymous function is called when the file has completed its download and always after the code that created the promise has exited.

The first value returned by the promise is the contents of the file as a string.

One of the problems with trying to find out what functions return as their final result is that usually the documentation just gives the fact they return a promise object with no mention of what the values are.

In jQuery what is passed to an onComplete, onError or onProgress function is determined by the asynchronous function that returns the promise object. It can return multiple values. In the case of the AJAX methods it returns a set of values corresponding to the properties of the jqXHR object in the order they are documented.

A JavaScript standard promise always only returns a single value, a jQuery promise can return multiple values.

Also, although you can write the code as above with the then method called later, it is usual to not store the promise object and simply call the then method as in:

```
$.get("TextFile.txt").then(
                     function (value) {
                       console.log(value);
                     });
```

It is also worth remembering that the functions defined within a then method are closures and so have access to the variables that are in scope at the point at which the function is defined.

In fact the get method doesn't return a promise object but a mix-in, a jqXHR object, that is partially the original object that get used to return, and partially a promise object. This allows more flexibility than just returning a promise object and it is one of the strengths of JavaScript's approach to object-oriented programming – but it can be confusing.

# Chaining Promises

At the moment it looks as if a promise is just another way to write callbacks. After all what is the difference between writing

```
slowFun(args,successCallback,errorCallback);
```

and

```
slowFun(args).then(successCallback,errorCallback);
```

Looked at in this way there is no real difference and if it helps you understand the way promises work then by all means think about then as just another way to write callbacks. However, there is a little more sophistication here that you might think and its all to do with the idiom of chaining functions.

A particular problem with asynchronous tasks is to arrange that taskB is only started when taskA has completed. In Chapter 3 we looked at various ways of achieving this including the use of jQuery's function queue. Promises provide yet another and arguably the best way of doing this.

If you want to perform two asynchronous tasks, one after the other, you can by simply chaining then method calls. As in all function chaining to make it work you have to return the correct sort of object from each function and in this case its another promise.

In many ways this idea is key to understanding and using promises in more sophisticated ways.

To understand what is going on we need to master one subtle point of the way promises work.

**The then method always immediately returns a promise object.**

*Note: This is not always the way then used to work in jQuery. The* then *function was implemented in a nonstandard way and this was the source of the criticism of jQuery's promises. In jQuery 3* then *works correctly and this is what is described here. It isn't worth learning the wrong way to do this so if you have to cope with legacy code check the documentations.*

You can think of this as a default object returned to make sure you can always chain calls on the then function. This default promise has as its value  the value returned by the onComplete function of the original promise object.

For example:

```
var myPromise1 = $.get("TextFile.txt");

var myPromise2=myPromise1.then(
      function (value) {
        console.log(value);
        return "Hello";
      });

myPromise2.then(
      function (value) {
        console.log(value);
      });
```

The get function returns a promise object which we can use to set an onComplete using then. However, then also returns a promise object which can have an onComplete which will be called when it is resolved. The value of the promise is whatever the first onComplete returns.

If you run this you will see the contents of the file followed by "Hello" displayed in the console.

It is important that you really understand this example.

The key is to realize that myPromise1 and myPromise2 are returned at once by the get and the then. This is always the case because it is what allows the code to continue executing and run to completion.

At some time in the future after the code has completed the file finishes loading and myPromise1 is fulfilled and the onComplete function is fired with the promise's value i.e. the contents of the text file. It then returns "Hello" which is the value that myPromise2 has been waiting for and it and calls its onComplete function.

Of course this isn't how this code would generally be written. You can write it using the chaining or fluent style:

```
$.get("TextFile.txt");
    .then(
         function (value) {
           console.log(value);
           return "Hello";
        })
      .then(
         function (value) {
           console.log(value);
        });
```

This is neater and more compact but it is harder to see what promise object are in play.

What is the advantage of then returning a promise?

To see the advantage you have to think what if the first onComplete function was another slow operation?

In this case it should return a promise object so that the UI thread could get on with other things and not be held up by the onComplete function.

The rule is that if an onComplete function returns a value then it is the promise's value, but if it returns a promise then that promise's value is forwarded to the default promise as its value.

That is:

- If a promise is fulfilled by a normal i.e. non-promise value then the promise is fulfilled.
- If a promise is fulfilled by another promise then it isn't fulfilled until the second promise is and so on..

For example, suppose we need to download two files one after the other, we might use:

```
var myPromise1 = $.get("TextFile1.txt");
var myPromise2= myPromise1
  .then(
      function (value) {
        console.log(value);
        return $.get("TextFile2.txt");
      });
myPromise2.then(
      function (value) {
        console.log(value);
      })
```

What happens is almost identical to the previous example.

The get immediately returns myPromise1 and starts to download the file. Next the then immediately returns myPromise2 and sets up the onComplete callback.

The code then comes to an end freeing up the UI thread. At some time later the file finishes loading and this resolves myPromise1 with a value equal to the contents of the file. This causes the onComplete to start running which prints the contents of the file and starts the second download working.

The second get immediately returns a promise which is pending i.e unresolved and starts to download the second file. MyPromise2 continues to wait because the promise it has been supplied with is unresolved. MyPromise2 can only resolve if the supplied promise is resolved, they are both waiting on the value to become available.

Eventually the second file is downloaded and the promise returned by the get is resolved and this provides a value for MyPromise2 and it too is resolved.

Finally MyPromise2's onComplete is called and displays the value i.e. the contents of the second file.

What happens when a promise is returned to a promise is the trickiest part of understanding promises. But if you think of a simple promise as waiting for a value to be available, then a promise that is waiting for a promise is waiting for the same final value:

```
promise1 -waiting> promise2 -waiting> value
```

when promise 2 gets the value it resolves and passes the value back to promise 1 which is also resolved. The principle extends to more than two promises and you can have a chain of promises all waiting for the final one in the chain to resolve.

Of course, you might well want to download both files at the same time, but if you care about the order of downloading and need the first file to finish downloading before the second even starts, this is the way to do it.

Without using promises the only way to make sure that asynchronous functions occur one after another is to nest callbacks or you could use a function queue as described in Chapter 3.

Chaining promises is a fundamental way to order asynchronous tasks.

This is to be preferred to nested promises which is the promise analog of nesting callbacks e.g.:

```
var myPromise = $.get("TextFile1.txt");
myPromise.then(
   function (value) {
                   console.log(value);
                   $.get("TextFile2.txt").then(
                            function (value) {
                                console.log(value);
                            })
   })
```

This nests a callback within a callback. It is better to return the promise object and write things like:

```
object.then(oncomplete1).then(oncomplete2)
```

and so on.

The important point is:

**if you chain promises or asynchronous functions using then they are executed sequentially.**

Notice that to get things to happen in parallel you have to avoid chaining. For example to download the two files at the same time you would use:

```
var myPromise1 = $.get("TextFile1.txt");
myPromise1.then(
      function (value) {
        console.log(value);
      });

var myPromise2=$.get("TextFile2.txt");
myPromise2.then(
      function (value) {
        console.log(value);
       })
```

or just

```
$.get("TextFile1.txt").then(
      function (value) {
        console.log(value);

      });
$.get("TextFile2.txt").then(
      function (value) {
        console.log(value);
       })
```

Notice no chaining.

Also notice that if you want to add additional handlers to the same promise you can't use chaining. That is:

```
mypromise.then(onComplete1);
mypromise.then(onComplete2);
```

adds onComplete1 and onComplete2 to mypromise so that they will be executed when it is fulfilled. Both onComplete functions are passed the value of mypromise i.e. the same value. However,:

```
mypromise.then(onComplete1).then(onComplete2);
```

seems to do the same thing but onComplete1 is a called by mypromise with its value and onComplete2 is called by the promise returned by the `then` and its value is whatever onComplete1 returns.

## Using Named Functions

There is a tendency in JavaScript to always use anonymous functions because they seem to fit in with the flow of control you are trying to express. Hence it is typical to write:

```
$.get("TextFile1.txt")
  .then(
    function (value) {
      console.log(value);
      return $.get("TextFile2.txt");
    },
    function(error){
      handle the error
    })
  .then(
    function (value) {
     console.log(value);
    },
    function(error){
     handle the error
    });
```

However, there are significant downsides to using anonymous functions. In particular error reporting doesn't include the name of a function on the stack and there is no clue as to what the function is trying to do. Compare the above with:

```
$.get("TextFile1.txt")
 .then(processFirstFile,handleError1 )
 .then(processSecondFile,handleError2)
```

Also notice that as you have to pass the functions as references you don't include the parameters. If you did, i.e. if you wrote:

```
 .then(processFirstFile(value),handleError1(error) )
```

then the functions would be called at once and not when the promise was settled. The parameters are in the definition of the functions not when you pass them within a call to then.

Using named functions is arguably much easier to understand and with more appropriate function names it would be even easier. Of course the cost of this is that you have to define the functions earlier in the program but this is worth it because it provides a more modular approach.

**Using named functions makes promises easier to understand.**

## Combining Promises

If you have a set of asynchronous tasks that occur one after the other then you need to chain together their promise objects.

However, it is more common to have a set of asynchronous tasks that you want to set running, in parallel if possible, and then do something after they have all completed. In this case what you really need to do is join or combine all the promise objects together into one promise object that is resolved only when all of the original promise objects are resolved.

You can combine promises in this way using the when method. If you specify a list of promise objects in the call to when, it returns a single "master" promise object that is only resolved when all of the parameter promise objects are resolved.

The onComplete of the master promise object is passed all of the values that the parameter promise objects return.

If any of the parameter promise objects fail and are rejected then the master promise object fails. This means you could have some promise objects that are still working when the master promise object fails.

As a simple example consider downloading two files:

```
var myPromise1 = $.get("TextFile1.txt");
var myPromise2 = $.get("TextFile2.txt");
myTotalPromise = $.when(myPromise1, myPromise2);
myTotalPromise.then(
  function (value1,value2) {
    console.log(value1)
    console.log(value2);
 })
```

If you run this example you will discover that the two values returned by myPromise1 and mPromise2 are complete objects with all of the values returned by each promise - this is general behavior for the when method.

Notice also that you may well have to keep references to the promises that have been combined so that you can clean up after any tasks that fail. The general rule is that asynchronous processes are much harder to deal with when one fails than when they all work.

*Note: The promise standard uses all rather than when. The big difference is that you can pass it an array of promises and it supplies an array of values to the combined onComplete function.*

The when function will wait until all of the promises are resolved or at least one is rejected.

## First Promise To Resolve and More!

The when function solves the problem of waiting until all of the promises in a set resolve or at least one is rejected. You can think of this is the opposite of waiting for all of the promises to resolve. For standard JavaScript promises there is a function that does this - race. It will resolve when any one of the promises resolves. The problem is that you not only get the first success you also might well get the first rejection. This isn't usually what you want. In most cases you want to try a set of alternatives and take the first that is successful not the first that completes successfully or rejects.

An even bigger problem is that usually there is no way to abort the unfinished tasks corresponding to the promises that weren't first.

If you do want to do anything like "first promise to return a valid result" then you can cast the jQuery promise into a JavaScript promise and use the race function. To convert a jQuery promise to a JavaScript promise all you have to do is:

```
var JavaScript=Promise.resolve(jQueryPromise);
```

After this you can use the JavaScript Promise in place of the jQuery one including the race function.

However, in most cases you need something more specific to the task in hand. For example you need the first result that is successful. In this case you have no choice but to write the logic yourself.

There are lots of other possibilities.

You could ask for a function that returns the last promise to complete successfully so you could find out how many had worked or failed. You could ask for a function that that returned the last to fail, and so on, the combinations are obvious.

Rather than provide a set of functions that martial promises in this way it is better to learn how to create your own so that you can build in your own exact requirements and this is something covered in the next chapter.

## Other Promise Methods

Most of the time you can get the job done using just the then method of the promise object but jQuery does provide some extras which are mostly historical and to be avoided.

Instead of using the then method to define what should happen you can use the **done**, **fail** or **always** methods to add functions to the promise object which are carried out when the task completes, fails or when the task either completes or fails.

For example, the previous example could be written:

```
var myPromise = $.get("TextFile.txt");
myPromise.done(
 function (value) {
  console.log(value);
 });
```

All three functions can accept any number of functions, or an array of functions, to execute when the promise is resolved.

The big problem with the `done`, `fail` and `always` is that they do not chain like `then`. They return the first promise and this means you cannot use them to execute promises sequentially.

So for example, if you try the original sequential file download but using `done` rather than `then`:

```
var myPromise1 = $.get("TextFile1.txt");
var myPromise2= myPromise1
   .done(
     function (value) {
       console.log(value);
       return $.get("TextFile2.txt");
     });
myPromise2.done(
     function (value) {
       console.log(value);
     })
```

You will find that you get the contents of TextFile1.txt displayed on the console twice, not the first file followed by the second. The reason that this doesn't work is that `done` doesn't return a new promise but the original promise. That is in the program above myPromise1 is the same as myPromise2.

There might be special cases where `done, fail` and `always` provide the correct behavior but they do not work in the way you would expect from a standard promise.

There is an argument that always is useful at the end of a chain as a default clean up function because after the final always the chain comes to an end. For this reason it isn't a function to avoid completely, however:

**Avoid done and fail and use then instead.**

Also avoid using `pipe` which was originally provided to give the same behavior as then and is now deprecated.

Finally the `state` function can be used to discover the state of a promise - pending, resolved or rejected. This isn't often useful.

# Promise Error Handling

One of the big advantages of using promises is that they make error handling easier. Not easy, but easier. Asynchronous error handling is never easy because errors can occur in a function while other functions are still executing. There is generally no way of canceling asynchronous functions and this can make it difficult to work out what to do. However, the main problem promises solve is detecting when something has gone wrong.

We already know that you can specify an error handler as part of the then function.

```
$.get("TextFile1.txt").then(processFirstFile(value),
                            handleError1(error));
```

The handleError function will be called if the get fails for any reason i.e. if it returns an error status.

This is simple but things get a little more complicated when we have a chain of thens. If you are running one asynchronous task after another then we have already discovered that you can do this by a chaining thens.

For example:

```
var promise2=promise1.then(onSuccess1,onFailure1);
```

where chaining has been avoided to show the explicit promises returned. The first then returns promise2 that is settled when onSuccess1 returns a value or a settled promise.

It is also helpful to keep in mind that in say:

```
var promise2=promise1.then(onSuccess1,onFailure1);
```

It is the settlement state of promise1 that determines which of onSuccess1 or onFailure1 are executed and what onSuccess1 or onFailure1 return that determines the settlement state of promise2.

However, there is an additional rule governing chained promises. If there is no onSuccess or onFailure to handle the settlement of the promise then that state is passed to the next promise and so on until there is a handler for the state.

**That is an unhandled state is passed to the next promise in the chain.**

This intentionally copies the way that exceptions work in synchronous code.

So for example if we have, writing the chain out in full for clarity:

```
var promise2=promise1.then(null,onFailure1);
var promise3=promise2.then(onSuccess2,onFailure2);
```

and promise1 is fulfilled there is no onSuccess handler defined in its then. What happens is that this state is passed to promise2 which is fulfilled and onSuccess2 is executed. Notice that the final state of promise2 would have been determined by the missing onSuccess1 handler so passing the state on is reasonable as a default.

The same rule applies to the rejection handlers. If there is no rejection handler and the promise is rejected then that state is passed to the next handler in the chain.

Once the state has found a handler then processing resumes its normal course.

But to make sense of "normal course" we need one final rule.

Any handler that returns a value and does not throw an error passes on a success to the next promise and this includes onFailure handlers. Any handler that throws an exception passes a reject on to the next promise.

This all seems complicated but the rule is that states are passed on if there is no handler for the state, and any handler that returns a value and doesn't throw an exception passes on a success to the next promise.

For example:

```
var promise2=promise1.then(onSuccess1);
var promise3=promise2.then(onSuccess2,onFailure2);
var promise4=promise3.then(onSuccess3);
```

which would normally be written:

```
promise1.then(onSuccess1)
        .then(onSuccess2,onFailure2)
        .then(onSuccess3);
```

Suppose promise1 is rejected then as it has no onFailure handler, the rejection is passed on to promise2 which causes onFailure2 to run. Assuming onFailure2 returns a value and doesn't throw an exception then promise3 is fulfilled and onSuccess3 runs. You can think of this as a successful run of onFailure2 keeps the sequence of operations going. If this isn't what you want then throw an exception in onFailure1.

In most cases it is reasonable to leave any rejection of any promise in a chain of promises till the very end so aborting the chain.

For example:

```
var promise2=promise1.then(onSuccess1);
var promise3=promise2.then(onSuccess2);
var promise4=promise3.then(onSuccess3);
var promise5=promise4.then(null,onFailure4);
```

If any of the promises are rejected then the subsequent tasks are not started and the next function to be executed is onFailure4 which is a catch all error routine.

This is such a common idiom that there is a special `catch` function which just sets a reject handler. So you could write the above as:

```
var promise2=promise1.then(onSuccess1);
var promise3=promise2.then(onSuccess2);
var promise4=promise3.then(onSuccess3);
var promise5=promise4.catch(onFailure4);
```

Of course even this isn't the usual way to write this because we use chaining:

```
promise1.then(onSuccess1)
        .then(onSuccess2)
        .then(onSuccess3)
        .catch(onFailure4);
```

which now looks a lot more like the synchronous try-catch block that it models. To be clear if there is a problem in any of the tasks say in onSuccess2 then effectively control jumps straight to onFailure4.

There are lots and lots of situations in which you can use promises that we haven't looked at. A general programming feature like promises are capable of very varied use and a full catalog is very likely impossible. However, if you understand how they work, you should be able to work out how promises behave in any given situation.

# Summary

- Instead of accepting callbacks, asynchronous functions can and do return promises.

- You can add the equivalent of onComplete and onError callbacks to the promise using the then function.

- You can convert a jQuery promise to a JavaScript promise using:
  var JavaScript=Promise.resolve(jQueryPromise);
  However, this isn't usually necessary as jQuery promises are standards compatible.

- A promise object is in one of three states. When it is first created it is pending. If the task ends correctly then it is in the resolved or fulfilled state. If the task ends with an error it enters the rejected state.

- A promise is also said to be settled if it isn't pending. When a promise is settled it cannot thereafter change its state.

- Handlers are called asynchronously when the promise is settled. Any handlers that are added after the promise is settled are also called asynchronously.

- The then function returns a new promise which is fulfilled if its onComplete handler returns a value. If its onComplete handler returns a promise, this promise determines the state of the promise returned by the then.

- Notice that in a chain of promises the fulfillment state of a promise determines which of the handlers it then executes and the result of the handler determines the state of the promise that the then returned.

- If a suitable handler isn't defined for the promise then its state is passed on to the next promise in the chain in lieu of the state that would have been determined by the missing handler.

- If a handler doesn't throw an exception then the fulfilled state is passed on to the next promise in the chain. That is if the handler doesn't return a promise then as long as it hasn't thrown an exception the next promise is fulfilled.

- If a handler throws an exception then the next promise in the chain is rejected.

- The catch function can be used to define an onError handler - it is equivalent to then(null,onError).

# Chapter 6

# Implementing Promises

Promises are new and this means that there are asynchronous functions that don't make use of them. This leads on to the need to promisify existing and future code. To do this you need to know a little about how promises work internally and how to make them do what you want.

After learning how to use or consume promises the next step is to add support for promises to asynchronous functions and to work with them to create new promise features.

## The jQuery Deferred Object

The big problem initially in implementing promises was that it was essential to provide functions so that the code that was using the promise to signal when it was finished could change the state of the promise, but code that was consuming the promise using then and catch functions was unable to change the promise's state.

That is:

**only the code that created the promise should be able to set the promise's state.**

The earliest solution to this problem of keeping the internal state private was to use a two-object solution. A deferred object was used by the promise creator to manage the promise. The Deferred had the necessary functions to resolve and reject the promise and the promise had all of the functions the consumer needed, like then. In practice it was better to have the deferred object also having all of the functions that the promise had and so the deferred looked like a "super" promise object.

In retrospect this is probably a mistake as it results in a confusion between what the deferred is and what it is used for. If you wanted to you could pass the deferred object to the user rather than the promise and this would allow them to change the internal state.

To summarize:

- The `deferred` object has all of the properties and methods of a promise and some additional methods that allow you to change the state of the promise associated with it.
- The `deferred` object is used by the code that creates and manipulates the promise.
- That code should return only the associated promise to its clients so that they can use the then and similar methods but not affect the promise's state.

You create a `deferred` using:

```
var def=$.Deferred();
```

The most important `deferred` methods are:

```
resolve/reject
resolveWith/rejectWith
```

In most cases you will use resolve or reject.

If you call a `deferred` resolve method then the promise associated with it is fulfilled. That is, any onComplete handler attached using `then` will be called with the same arguments.

For example

```
def.resolve(myValue);
```

sets the promises state to fulfilled which results in any `then` onComplete handler to be called with myValue as a parameter.

The reject method works in the same way but it causes the promise to be rejected.

For example:

```
def.reject(myReason);
```

sets the promise's state to rejected and any failure callback is called with myReason as a parameter.

Notice that both the resolve and reject methods are different from JavaScript standard promises which only allow a single argument to be passed. If you want to be compatible with the promise standard than only pass a single parameter in resolve or reject. If you have multiple values you need to pass then create an object with them as properties and pass the single object.

The functions resolveWith and rejectWith work in the same way as resolve and reject, but the first argument sets the context, i.e. this in the calls of the onSuccess or onReject handlers.

So for example:

```
def.resolveWith(myButton,myValue);
```

will set the promise's state to fulfilled and call any onSuccess handler with myValue as a parameter and with this set to myButton. It isn't often that you need resolveWith or rejectWith, but they can make using object methods as promise handlers possible.

The only other deferred function that is important is promise which returns a reference to the promise that the deferred is associated with.

## Using a Deferred

One of the problems of using Deferreds is seeing how they are actually used to implement an asynchronous function that returns and manages a promise. The best way of finding out is by way of a simple example.

The timeOut function has already been introduced in earlier chapters as a way of turning a synchronous function into an asynchronous one. It can also be used to delay the running of a function by a specified time:

```
timeOut(function,time);
```

will run the specified function after time milliseconds have past. We can turn this into a delay function that returns a promise that resolves after the specified time.

All we have to do is create a deferred:

```
function delay(t) {
    var d = $.Deferred();
```

Next we start the asynchronous operation off and arrange that when it is finished it sets the Deferred's state to fulfilled or rejected. In this case it is difficult to see how the timer could fail and so we just need to fulfill the Deferred when the time is up:

```
setTimeout(
          function () {
            d.resolve();
          }, t);
```

Now all we have to do is return the promise so that the client code can use it:

```
return d.promise();
}
```

That's it!

The complete function is:

```
function delay(t) {
  var d = $.Deferred();
  setTimeout(
            function () {
              d.resolve();
            }, t);
  return d.promise();
}
```

If this is your first promise-returning function you might think it is strange - where is the function that is run when the delay is up?

The whole point is that this function will delay running any function the client code associates with it using then and it will run multiple functions if you want it to. For example, to use it you might write:

```
delay(1000).then(
            function () {
              console.log("time up");
            });
```

As delay returns a promise, you can use any of the usual methods to schedule other functions depending on its state - primarily then and catch, but this is trickier than it might seem, as described later.

## JavaScript Promises

Now that you have seen how Deferred works it is much easier to see how the JavaScript standard promise works. The reason we have a Deferred object, as well as a promise object, in jQuery is that we need to keep resolve and reject private and this is achieved in jQuery by making them methods of another object. In the promises standard both resolve and reject are private methods of the promise object itself.

A private method is one that is created as a closure when an object is created. This is the standard method for creating a private variable accessible from within an object but not from outside. The only difference is that the variable references a function. For example:

```
function myConstructor(){
 var private=0;
 this.myFunction=function(){
                    alert(private);
                  }
}
```

This is a constructor for an object with just one method, myFunction.

The important part is the variable called private. This is not part of the object because it isn't declared as a property of the object. so if you try:

```
var myObject=new myConstructor();
myObject.private=1;
```

you will see an error that private doesn't exist. However, as private is in scope when myFunction is declared, it is available to it as a closure. That is:

```
myObject.myFunction();
```

does display the value of private.

A private method uses the same mechanism with the small difference that the variable references a function.

This is the mechanism that the JavaScript promise uses to make resolve and reject private methods. When you create a standard promise you use its constructor and you pass it a function that is immediately executed by the constructor. This is the function where you create the asynchronous task and then call resolve or reject accordingly. In other words this is the code that does the work.

For example the delay function example can be written using JavaScript promises as:

```
function delay(t) {
 var p = new Promise(
             function (resolve, reject) {
               setTimeout(
                 function () {
                   resolve();
                 }, t);
             });
 return p
}
```

You can see that it has the same basic structure, the only difference is that now the code that calls the private resolve and reject functions is passed to the constructor. The constructor executes this immediately and returns the promise.

## jQuery or JavaScript Promise?

Now that you have seen the way Deferred and the JavaScript promise object work, you can appreciate that there isn't much difference. This raises the question of which one should you use?

If you are consuming promises then you can just live with whichever type of promise you are returned. For example, if you use jQuery's JSONget then it returns a jQuery promise that you can use as if it was a JavaScript promise.

On the other hand, if you are adding promise support to a function then it makes sense to use JavaScript promises as this is the way of the future and your new promisified function will still work with jQuery.

The only reason to prefer jQuery's Deferred is if you want to support browsers that don't have the latest version of JavaScript and that mainly comes down to any version of IE. jQuery 3 supports IE 9+ and if you try the delay function out in both versions you will discover that the jQuery version works on IE 11, say, but the JavaScript promise version fails with a Promise object not defined error.

Given that IE 11 still has a 4% market share  at the time of writing, you might want to consider using jQuery Deferred. When IE has a small enough market share to ignore, converting to using JavaScript promises would be an easy task.

## The Then Parameter Problem

As delay now returns a promise, it seems obvious that it could be used in a chain (see the previous chapter). However, there is a problem.

If you try:

```
getTime();
delay(1000)
  .then(getTime)
   .then(delay(1000))
    .then(getTime);
```

where getTime is something like:

```
function getTime() {
  var time = new Date().getTime();
  console.log(time);
}
```

which shows a timer count in milliseconds, what you discover is that it appears to work, but if you look carefully the getTime functions report times that are only a few milliseconds apart, rather than 1000ms apart.

The reason should be easy to spot. The functions that are being passed to the then function have parameters and this means they are evaluated at once and not passed to the then to be activated at a later time.

**The problem is that you cannot pass a parameter to a function that you use in a then.**

Notice that when it is called by the promise, the function may be passed any number of parameters depending on the way the promise is settled.

There are a number of solutions to the problem, but none are 100% satisfactory.

The first, and most obvious, is not to use a parameter at all, but this would result in a delay function that gave a fixed time delay and this generally isn't what you want.

The second is to use a technique from functional programming called "currying" to reduce the number of parameters in the function. For example:

```
getTime();
delay(1000)
   .then(getTime)
   .then(function(){return delay(1000);})
   .then(getTime);
```

In this case we have used the anonymous function to curry the delay function, i.e. we have reduced the number of parameters to zero. If you try this you will find that it works and each of the times is roughly 1000ms apart.

You can take this one-off currying and create a function that will automatically curry delay for you, for example:

```
function delay(t) {
   return function () {
           var d = $.Deferred();
           setTimeout(
              function () {
                 d.resolve(0);
              }, t);
           return d.promise();
        };
}
```

You can see that this is the same idea, but now the delay function returns a function that delays for t milliseconds with no parameters. With this version of delay you can use:

```
getTime();
delay(1000)()
   .then(getTime)
    .then(delay(1000))
     .then(getTime);
```

The extra parentheses following the first use of delay are not a misprint. The delay function returns a function that delays for t milliseconds and to implement the delay it has to be called.

The need for the double pairs of parentheses is not nice, but there seems to be no way that a function that returns a promise and accepts parameters can be used in the same way outside and inside a then.

The final way of doing the job is to use bind to curry the delay function. The bind function returns another function with a specified context and fixed values for any of its parameters. Using the original delay function we can call it in a then using:

```
getTime();
delay(1000)
  .then(getTime)
   .then( delay.bind(null,1000))
    .then(getTime);
```

The `bind` returns a function with the call context set to null and the first parameter set to 1000. The call to `bind` is reputed to be slow.

Of the solutions, probably the best, is to write the function using a parameter and remember to wrap it in an anonymous currying function if you use it in a then:

```
.then(function(){return delay(1000);})
```

This is one of the negative features of using promises. You have to remember that a function that returns a promise can have parameters, but you cannot specify these parameters when you use the function in a then unless you use currying or something similar.

## Composing Promises

One of the more advanced aspects of using promises is writing functions that work with multiple promises in various ways. Many promise libraries provide utilities such as any, which is fulfilled if any promise is, some, fulfilled if a fixed number of promises are and so on. The JavaScript promise standard provides just two

- `all` fulfilled if all are
- `race` fulfilled if one is

The jQuery Deferred only provides `all`.

Rather than providing lots of different standard promise-composing functions, it is simpler to learn how to write your own that do exactly what you want. Usually the problem is how to handle rejects, and this you can tailor to the situation.

As an example, let's implement a simple version of the race function which returns a promise that resolves when the first of two promises resolve. It is always a good idea to try to implement an idea as simply as possible and then extend it to more realistic examples.

It turns out that race is very easy to write:

```
function race(p1,p2){
 var d = $.Deferred();
 p1.then(function(value){d.resolve(value);},
         function(error){d.reject(error);}
        );
 p2.then(function(value){d.resolve(value);},
         function(error){d.reject(error); }
        );
 return d.promise();
}
```

All that happens is that we return a new promise object that is resolved or rejected when any of the promises provided as arguments resolves or rejects. Notice that we don't do anything to stop the other promises from completing. It is generally difficult to cancel a pending asynchronous operation. Also notice that as a promise is immutable we don't need to worry about later promises settling and trying to set the returned promise to something different.

This can be used to get the first promise to resolve or reject:

```
getTime();
race([delay(1000), delay(2000)]).then(getTime);
```

In this case you will see a delay of 1000ms.

Of course, you could add the race function as a method to the promise object.

Extending the race function to work with any number of promises can be done in two ways, either jQuery's multiple parameters or JavaScript's iterable. In practice both are very similar to implement.

To implement the jQuery approach we simply use the arguments array:

```
function race() {
 var d = $.Deferred();
 $.map(arguments,
         function (p) {
            p.then(function (value) {
                  d.resolve(value);
               },
               function (error) {
                  d.reject(error);
               });
         });
 return d.promise();
}
```

You can see the general idea. For each promise in the arguments array we use then to attach a resolve and reject handler. This version can be called as before with separate arguments. To implement the JavaScript version we simply have to include an explicit array parameter and alter the way the function is called:

```
function race(args) {
 var d = $.Deferred();
 $.map(args,
         function (p) {
            p.then(function (value) {
                     d.resolve(value);
                  },
                  function (error) {
                     d.reject(error);
                  });
         });
 return d.promise();
}
```

and to call the function:

```
getTime();
race([delay(1000), delay(2000)]).then(getTime);
```

Notice that now there is a single array parameter.

Of the two, I think I prefer the arguments approach used by jQuery.

This is an implementation of the standard race function, but it is generally held that it isn't very useful as it will return the first function to complete, even if it rejects. What would be better is an implementation of any, which is found in some promise libraries, that returns the first successful result or a reject if there is no successful function:

```
function any() {
 var d = $.Deferred();
 var number = arguments.length;
 $.map(arguments, function (p) {
                     p.then(function (value) {
                           d.resolve(value);
                        },
                        function (error) {
                           if (--number === 0) {
                              d.reject(error);
                           }
                        });
                  });
 return d.promise();
}
```

This works in a very similar way to race but we now maintain a count of the number of promises included in the arguments. Each time a promise is rejected we reduce the count by one. If the count reaches zero then all of the promises have been rejected and we change the state of the returned promise to rejected. Notice that as long as one of the promises resolves the returned promise resolves. As before, we make no attempt to cancel any no longer wanted promises or tasks.

As a final example, and one that is useful in practice, let's explore a timeOut function. One of the problems with promises is that they don't have a timeout. If a promise isn't resolved or rejected then it will continue to be pending forever. The following function takes a promise and returns a new promise that will reject if the original promise doesn't accept or reject within the specified timeout:

```
function timeOut(p, t) {
 var d = $.Deferred();
 p.then(function (value) {
         d.resolve(value)
       },
       function (error) {
         d.reject(error)
       });
 setTimeout(function () {
             d.reject("timeout");
           },t);
 return d.promise();
}
```

Again, this is very simple. All that happens is that a new Deferred is created and is resolved if the original promise resolves and is rejected if the setTimeout is triggered first. This would be easier to use as a method added to the promise object because then it could be used with chaining.

## Beyond Promises

Once you understand the way promises can be used to trigger other promises the only problem is that you will go too far with the idea. Keep it simple and only write the code you actually need. Promises are a reasonably good solution to the asynchronous problem, but the soon to be common async and await is so much better. Promises are a solution for now, but not for the longer term future.

# Summary

- Only the code that created the promise should be able to set the promise's state. The earliest solution to this problem of keeping the internal state private was to use a two-object solution. A Deferred object was used by the promise creator to manage the promise.

- A Deferred object has resolve and reject methods that change the state of its associated promise object.

- To use a Deferred you should create it and allow your asynchronous code to use resolve and reject when it completes and return a promise object to the client code.

- JavaScript standard promises keep the resolve and reject private without the use of a management object, i.e. a Deferred. Instead they provide resolve and reject as private functions that can be accessed via the constructor.

- To create a standard promise you pass the constructor a function with resolve and reject as parameters. The code in the function runs the asynchronous task and calls either resolve or reject when the task finishes. The constructor calls the function immediately and this provides access to the private resolve and reject methods.

- If you are consuming promises provided by other software, jQuery in particular, there is little reason to convert whatever flavor of promise is being used to a JavaScript standard promise.

- If you are creating functions that return promises then use JavaScript standard promises unless you need to support IE when jQuery Deferreds are preferable.

- It seems natural to create functions with parameters that return promises but these are difficult to use in a then because of the need to pass a reference and not execute the function. The standard solution is to use currying to set the parameters.

- It is easy to create a range of functions that combine a set of promises into a single promise that is resolved when some subset of the original promises are.

# Chapter 7

# Web Workers and Promises

It is fairly easy to consume promises returned by asynchronous functions that other programmers have put together for you. It is only a little more difficult to use promises to create your own asynchronous functions that run in parallel with a non-UI thread.

It is assumed that you already know about jQuery's Deferred and promise objects. If not read the previous two chapters.

## Custom Async With a Single Thread

So far we have used promises to make existing asynchronous features like AJAX easier to work with. We have also looked at how to create our own custom asynchronous functions. However, these don't really have the same characteristics as the built-in asynchronous functions.

When you start an AJAX file transfer for example the UI thread is able to get on with other things while the system handles the file transfer and signals back when it is complete. That is in one way or another true asynchronous operations do involve other threads if only behind the scenes.

However, it is still possible to convert a potentially long running function into one that is executed on the UI thread in short bursts. For an example see the computePiAsync function as described in Chapter 3.

It is also possible and useful to use promises to make the function easier to use.

All it has to do is return a promise and call resolve when it has finished. It can also optionally use the notify function to return an intermediate result.

For example the computePiAsync function is easy to convert to use a promise and support notification:

```
function computePiAsync(end)
{
 var state = {};
 state.k = 0;
 state.pi = 0;
 var d = $.Deferred();

 function computePi() {
   if (state.k >= end) d.resolve(state);
   var i;
   for (i = 0; i < 1000; i++) {
     state.k++;
     state.pi += 4 * Math.pow(-1, state.k + 1) /(2 * state.k - 1);
   }
   d.notify(state);
   setTimeout(computePi, 0);
 }
 setTimeout(computePi, 0);
 return d.promise();
}
```

The first and main difference is that now we create a Deferred and return its associated promise. Notice that the computation is run until the total number of loops is equal to or greater than the end value specified and this results in the resolve function being called. The value passed back to the promise is that state object. It is a good idea to try and only pass back a single value to stay compatible with JavaScript promises. After each block of 1000 computations the notify method is called to pass the intermediate result back to the main program.

The main program would use the new promise returning version of the function something like:

```
var p = computePiAsync(100000);
p.progress(function (value) {
            $("#result").text(value.pi);
            $("#count").text(value.k);
          });
p.then(function (value) {
            $("#result").text(value.pi);
            $("#count").text("Final value " + value.k);
          });
```

You can see that the progress is displayed and a final value.

The same approach works for other long running operations.

- Keep the state in a state object and terminate the function after doing a small amount of work.
- Arrange to restart the function for the next block of work by using setTimeout with a delay of zero.
- Return a promise object and call notify at the end of each block and call resolve at the end for the entire calculation. If there is an error also remember to call reject.

## Web Worker Based Promises

The sort of asynchronous function we have just constructed is more like simulated async rather than the real thing. It is more like setting up a timeout event so that you can do some work in small chunks and not block the UI thread.

A second type of asynchronous programming that occurs in practice is where you use another thread of execution to complete a long running task while the UI thread gets on with what it is supposed to do i.e. look after the UI. For example, when you start an AJAX file download the operating system allocates another thread to look after the task. From the point of view of a JavaScript programmer it all seems magical. You ask for a file and some time later the file is available and all without the UI thread having to do anything at all. This is usually how we view asynchronous code in JavaScript but behind the scenes the OS is busy scheduling threads. You can think of the previous example of using setTimeout to schedule the running of a function as doing the scheduling job that OS takes on when you use another thread. However, there is also the very real possibility that the hardware supports multiple cores and the other thread might well be really running in parallel with the UI thread. That is, the OS can implement true parallel execution and this makes thing work faster.

Until recently there was no way that a JavaScript programmer could take advantage of the OS to schedule threads or of multiple cores to implement true parallelism but now we have the Web Worker which implements background processing on a non-UI thread.

There is no doubt that the best way to package a worker thread is as a promise. This isn't difficult but there are are some subtle points and it is easy to become confused.

To wrap a long running function that uses a worker thread as a promise, all we have to do is create a function that returns a promise object. The interesting thing is that the worker code doesn't generally need any changes to make use of a promise. It simply computes the answer or completes the task and then uses the postMessage method to trigger a message event on the UI thread and to return the result.

First we need to recap the basic principles of using a Web Worker.

## Basic Web Worker

The good news is that Web Worker is very easy to use.

What is slightly difficult to get to grips with  is working out what you are not allowed to do and achieving simple communication between the threads.

Ideally you should wrap any Web Worker tasks you create as promises to make the code easier to use. We will take a look at how to do this using jQuery later – for the moment let's concentrate on using Web Workers raw.

There really is only one key object when using Web Workers, the Worker object.

The worker object automatically starts a new thread and begins executing JavaScript code as soon as it is created.

The basic action is that it loads the JavaScript file that you specify in its constructor and starts the script executing on a new thread. It is possible to avoid using a separate file to store the code but it is messy and best avoided. The reason the code is in a separate file is to keep the execution contexts separated on the threads. That is, the program that starts on the new worker thread has no shared variables with the code that creates it.

So for example, if you have a program stored in myScript.js the instruction:

```
var worker=new Worker("myScript.js");
```

Although this is simple there is a subtlety that you need to get clear if you are to avoid making silly mistakes.

When you create a Worker object two things happen.

1. the code stored in myScript.js or whatever file you specify, is loaded and set running using a new OS level thread.

2. A Worker object is created on the UI thread and this is an object that your "standard" JavaScript code running on the UI thread can work with.

If you think that this is obvious and doesn't need to be said, so much the better.

## The Trouble With Threads

If you have looked at the problem of writing multi-threaded programs this is where you might be getting worried. Starting a new thread so easily seems to be an easy way to do something dangerous. However, Web Workers have been implemented in a way that restricts the way that you use them to make them safe. At first these restrictions might seem tough to live with, but after a while you realize that they are perfectly reasonable and don't really stop you from doing anything.

The main simplification about threading with Web Workers is that the new thread cannot share anything with the UI thread.

The new thread cannot access any objects that the UI Thread can. This means it cannot interact with any global objects and it cannot interact with the DOM or the user interface in any way. The new thread runs in a little world of its own – but don't panic as it can communicate with the UI thread in a very simple way.

This inability to share objects  may seem a little restrictive but it is a restriction that is necessary to make sure that the two threads you now have don't try to access the same object at the same time.

If this was allowed to happen you would need to introduce a lot of complicated machinery – locks, semaphores and so on – to make sure that the access was orderly and didn't give rise to any very difficult to find bugs – race conditions, deadlock and so on.

In other words the Web Worker has big restrictions so that you can use it without complication and without any danger.

For most purposes it is sufficient and hence very effective.

Web Workers do have access to all of the global core JavaScript objects that you might expect.

They can also access some functions that are normally associated with the DOM – XMLHttpRequest() and setInterval etc.

The rule is that if the object could be shared in anyway with the UI thread then you cannot get access to it and this is a condition that is obviously satisfied for all of the core JavaScript objects and the DOM objects that are allowed.

To make up for this restriction there are two new objects that the Web Worker can access - WorkerNavigator and WorkerLocation. The navigator provides basic information about the app's context - the browser in use, appName, appVersion and so on. The location object provides details of where the app is in terms of the current URL

if these two objects don't provide enough information you can easily arrange to pass the worker thread additional data of your choosing.

## Basic Communication Methods

So if the Web Worker is isolated from the UI thread how do the two communicate?

The answer is that they both use events and a method that causes events on the other thread.

### UI Thread To Worker Thread

Let's start with the UI thread sending a message to the worker thread. The Worker object that is created on the UI thread has a postMessage method which triggers a message event on the worker thread. Notice that this is where the thread crossover occurs. The Worker object is running on the UI thread but the event occurs in the code running on the worker thread.

For example:

```
var worker=new Worker("myScript.js");
worker.postMessage({mydata:"some data"});
```

The postMessage method triggers a message event in the worker code and sends it an event object that includes the data packaged as an object or an array.

To get the message sent to the Worker object you have to set up an event handler and retrieve the event object's data property.

For example, in the Web Worker code you would write:

```
this.addEventListener("message", function (event) {
```

In the Web Worker code the global context is provided by `this` or `self` and this gives access to all of the methods and objects documented. To get the message you would use:

```
var somedata = event.data.mydata;
```

Of course as you are passing an object to the event handler you could package as many data items as you needed to.

Notice that it is important to be very clear what is going on here. The postMessage method call is on the UI thread but the event handler is on the worker thread.

It is also important to realize that the data that is passed between the two threads isn't shared. A copy is made using the structured clone algorithm and it is this copy that the worker received. You can use a wide range of types of data to pass to the worker but if it is big the time taken to copy could be significant. If this is the case. you need to use a transferable object which is shared rather than copied.

## Worker Thread To UI Thread

Passing data from the worker thread to the UI thread works in exactly the same way – only the other way round. You use the postMessage method in the worker thread and attach an event handler for the message event in the UI thread.

For example, in the worker code:

```
this.postMessage({mydata:"some data"});
```

notice that in this case you can use `this` or `self` to call postMessage because you are running inside the Web Worker.

This triggers a message event in the UI thread and you can define a handler and retrieve the data using:

```
worker.addEventListener("message",
 function (e) {
   var somedata= e.data.mydata;
 });
```

Once again you have to be very clear that you understand what is running where. In this case the postMessage method is running on the worker thread and the event handler is running on the UI thread.

This is about all there is to using Web Workers.

There are some details about error handling and terminating the thread before it is complete but these are details. The general idea is that you use the message event to communicate between the two threads.

There is one subtle point that is worth keeping in mind. The events that you trigger in passing data between the two threads will happen in the order that you trigger them but they may not be handled promptly.

For example, if you start your worker thread doing an intensive calculation then triggering a "how are you doing" message event from the UI thread might not work as you expect. It could be that the worker thread is so occupied with its task that events are ignored until it reaches the end, and this is not what you might expect. The same happens with the messages passed from the worker thread but in this case the UI thread is generally not so focused on one task and so events usually get processed.

in general events going from the worker thread to the UI get processed as part of keeping the UI responsive. Events going the other way, i.e. from the UI thread to the worker, are not so reliable.

# A Simple Web Worker Example

As an example let's use the calculation of Pi example again. First we need a new JavaScript file called pi.js containing the following code:

```
var state = {};
state.k = 0;
state.pi = 0;
var i;
for (i = 0; i < 100000; i++) {
 state.k++;
 state.pi += 4 * Math.pow(-1, state.k + 1) / (2 * state.k - 1);
}
this.postMessage(state);
```

You can see that this worker is just a simple modification to the earlier program. The most important change is that we now no longer need to break the calculation up into chunks. As it is being performed on a separate thread it can run to completion and take as much time at it likes without any fear of blocking the UI – which is running on a different thread. When the calculation is complete it uses the postMessage method to fire a "message" event on the UI thread and supply the result.

The UI thread code is simply:

```
$("#button1").click(
            function (event) {
               $("#button1").prop("disabled", true);
               var worker = new Worker("pi.js");
               $(worker).on("message",
                         function (event) {
                  $("#result").text(event.originalEvent.data.pi);
                  $("#count").text(event.originalEvent.data.k);
                  $("#button1").prop("disabled", false);
               });
          });
```

Where we are using the UI of the previous example. Notice that we can use jQuery to work with the event handlers. The only small problem is that jQuery doesn't transfer the data field from the original Event object to its own and so we have to access it via originalEvent.

When the button is clicked the Worker constructor loads pi.js and starts it running on a new thread. The constructor returns a Worker object which runs on the UI thread in the variable worker.

When the worker thread is finished it fires the "message" event which is handled by the anonymous function which displays the result.

This is a very typical use of worker threads. The UI thread generally sends some data to initialize the worker thread and then simply waits for message events.

## Web Worker With Promises

Our next task is to make changes so that the asynchronous aspect of the worker is handled by a Promise object.

All of the new code is in the UI thread.

You can run jQuery on the worker thread but it isn't an easy task because jQuery expects to access the DOM and this isn't accessible from the worker thread.

We need to package the interaction between the UI thread and the worker as a function:

```
function piWorker() {
```

The first thing we need to do is create the Deferred object that eventually will be used to return a Promise object and to change the state of the Promise when everything is finished.

```
var d = $.Deferred();
```

The next thing we need to do is start the worker off:

```
var worker = Worker("worker.js");
```

Now we have a worker thread computing the result over some length of time and what we have to do to make sure that the UI is free to get on with its job is to bring this function to an end and return the promise object. However, this doesn't solve the problem of setting the promise object to resolved.

How can we do this so that the UI thread isn't blocked?

The answer is exactly as we have done it before – we set up an event handler for the message event:

```
$(worker).on("message",
            function (event) {
               d.resolve(event.originalEvent.data);
            });
```

Finally we return the promise object.

```
 return d.promise();
}
```

The complete code for the function is:

```
function piWorker() {
 var d = $.Deferred();
 var worker = new Worker("pi.js");
 $(worker).on("message",
               function (event) {
                 d.resolve(event.originalEvent.data);
               });
 return d.promise();
}
```

So how do we use the new function and the promise object it returns?

The answer is, as before, that you use it just like any other asynchronous function that returns a Promise.

```
$("#button1").click(
               function (event) {
                 $("#button1").prop("disabled", true);
                 piWorker().then(
                           function (value) {
                             $("#result").text(value.pi);
                             $("#count").text(value.k);
                             $("#button1").prop("disabled",false);
                           });
               });
```

The button's event handler now just has a simple call to the piWorker function and this immediately returns a promise object The then method of the promise object is used to define what should happen when the thread completes and returns the "promised" value. That is the function passed to then sets the button caption to the value and re-enables the button.

This is very much easier to use as the fact that we are using a separate thread is completely hidden from the client. In addition the client is able to define what is to be done with the result without having to delve into the inner workings of the function.

## Where Next?

Wrapping worker threads in a promise makes it easy for clients to make use of real asynchronous functions in JavaScript. While it might be difficult to use jQuery in the worker thread this is generally no disadvantage. When it comes to adding promises all of the work has to be done on the UI thread.

You can add error handling and periodic progress reports using the usual promise methods. You can also pass parameters to the worker thread to control it. Unusually you can even arrange to cancel the asynchronous operation because there is a terminate method that will dispose of a worker thread. However, as with all things, bringing a worker thread to a halt is usually more of a problem than you might imagine.

There are also lots of additional features of the worker thread that you might want to find out about including shared worker threads and transferable objects.

# Summary

- You can use promises to convert custom asynchronous functions running on the UI thread so that they are easier to use.

- Web Workers allow you to create true custom asynchronous functions/

- A worker thread cannot access any object that the UI thread can and vice versa. As a result there are many standard interfaces not available to a worker thread – most notably the DOM.

- The code for a worker thread has to be loaded from a file.

- The worker and UI thread communicate using the postMessage function which fires the message event in the other thread.

- You can pass a single item of data, which can be an object or an array, as an event parameter. A copy of the data object is passed to the other thread.

- It is easy to perform some calculations on the worker thread and pass a result back to  the UI thread to display.

- The idea way to encapsulate a function that invokes a worker thread is to use a promise. This allows the client to use `then` and `catch` to deal with the data or error returned.

# Chapter 8

# AJAX Basics - Get

AJAX is the technology that turned the web page into the web app. Since AJAX was invented there have been lots of innovations and frameworks that make web apps easier but a mastery of basic AJAX technique is still important and jQuery makes it easy and cross browser.

Wanting to make use of AJAX is one of the prime reasons for adopting jQuery. Working with AJAX raw in the browser isn't very difficult but exactly how it works varies according to the browser and jQuery does a very good job of covering up these differences. It isn't difficult to write JavaScript code that works in a wide range of browsers without jQuery but why bother when you get so much extra with jQuery.

First we have to deal with what exactly AJAX is all about and how we might use it.

Before AJAX, a web page loaded and then it loaded all of the resources, image files, JavaScript files and so on that it used. After the initial load there was no way a JavaScript program could download more data until the page was replaced by a new page. The web worked entirely in terms of whole pages and new behavior or new data from the server was download a whole page at a time.

The AJAX idea is to allow JavaScript to upload and download data to the server under program control. Web pages have always been able to upload data to the server using the HTML form mechanism but this has a limited but very useful applicability.

With AJAX you can, for example, download data from the server to a string say and then use it for whatever purpose you like. Often the new data is HTML which you can then use with jQuery to modify the DOM. In other words the page can be modified without the need to reload the entire page. This gives rise to the idea of the single page web app. A single HTML page can use JavaScript to update itself without ever having to load another page.

If you are planning to write a single page web app then there are frameworks that will make your task easier. You could do the whole job using nothing but jQuery and JavaScript but it would be a lot of work and you would have to reinvent the wheel many times.

jQuery AJAX isn't sufficient to build a complex one page web app. It is incredibly useful when you just need to augment an existing web page to have additional dynamic content.

Similarly you can get by using the standard HTML form to deliver data to the server in many cases. However, sometimes it is just more direct to handle the transfer of data yourself. The main reason for this is when the data doesn't originate in a simple user form.

The bottom line is that jQuery makes AJAX as easy as it can be for small tasks but for anything like a single page application or an MVC style website you need to look for and use a ready built framework.

In this chapter we start off by looking at the basic architecture of an HTTP request and introduce the simplest of jQuery's AJAX method – get.

Starting off with get means that we can avoid dealing with the complications of implementing a program on the server side. Our examples can simply retrieve a file stored on the server. For more complicated situations see the next chapter.

## AJAX From The Server's Point Of View

An HTML server only responds to a small number of request types. The only two transactions that are of any interest to AJAX are the Get and Post.

Get is the standard way a web page and other resources are delivered to a client browser. Without going into details, what happens is that the client puts together a get request with the URL of the resource it wants and the server finds the file corresponding to the path in the URL.

For example if the client does a get:

```
HTTP://myserver.com/myPage.html
```

then the server retrieves myPage.html from the local file system from the folder that is the root of the website and sends it to the client.

It really is that simple.

The Post is a little more tricky. When the client sends a Post request its sends a URL to the server and data consisting of name value pairs in the body of the HTTP message. In this case the web server isn't expected to return the web page corresponding to the URL to the user, but to use the web page to process the data. In fact the web page is returned to the client but if this is all that happened the data passed to the server would be ignored.

For example a Post to:

```
HTTP://myserver.com/myPage.html
```

does exactly the same as a Get to the same URL, i.e. it returns myPage.html to the client but a payload of data was delivered, and in this case, ignored by the server.

To be of any use the URL specified in a Post has to correspond to some sort of program that can process the data and optionally send a response back to the client. For example the URL often corresponds to a PHP web page which can access the data the server has received and send some HTML back to the client.

That is, the URL in a Post usually specifies a program that will accept the data from the client and send back a response.

*Note: if you are working with NetBeans and are trying things out with the embedded server it is important to know that its implementation of Post doesn't return a static file specified in the URL. However, it does work if you use the PHP embedded server.*

To summarize:

- Get – the server returns the specified file.
- Post – the server receives the specified data in the body of the HTTP request and returns the specified file.

Notice that it is also possible to pass the server data as part of the URL sent to the server – usually by using the query string. This works but it is limited in the amount of data that can be sent by the maximum length of a URL. For the moment we will ignore the query string approach to sending data to the server – see the next chapter for an example.

## jQuery Get

jQuery has an extensive and sophisticated set of AJAX methods but in many cases the "shortcut" methods are all you need as these perform the most common operations. However, this said there are often cases were you need the full AJAX method but let us start simple.

The most basic get method is:

```
$.get(url,function)
```

where the url is the resource you want to get and the function is the callback that is run if the request is successful.

For example to get the contents of a file called "mydata.txt" stored in the same directory as the current page you would use:

```
$.get("mydata.txt",
        function (data) {
          alert(data);
        });
```

The data contained in the file is passed to the callback function in the parameter – data in this case. When the AJAX call is complete the callback displays the data.

We have a lot to say about the data and the way it can be generated by the server but for the moment let's concentrate on the basics.

It turns out that including a callback as a parameter is the "old" way of doing things. Modern JavaScript and modern jQuery prefer to use Promises.

## Promises and AJAX

If this is as complicated as your AJAX use is and is going to be. then you can get away with simply using the callback form of get and the other AJAX methods. However, as demonstrated in earlier chapters promises are worth using if you are trying to build an asynchronous processing chain.

For the moment all you need to know is that all jQuery AJAX calls return an jqXHR object which is a super-set of a promise object - it is a promise with extras.

A promise object and hence a jqXHR object has two important methods:

**then**(doneFunction,failFunction) is used to set a function that is called when the AJAX task has completed successfully and a function that is called when the AJAX task fails for some reason.

**catch**(failFunction) is used to set a function that is called when the AJAX task has failed. It is equivalent to then(null,failFunction)

As all promise methods return a promise object you can chain method calls on a jqXHR object just as you would with a promise. There are many other methods that the jqXHR inherits from the promise but in most cases you shouldn't make use of them unless you have a really good reason to. For example, as explained in earlier chapters, the done function looks like an equivalent to then(function,null) but it isn't because it doesn't chain like the then and catch methods.

You can also use the **always** function which runs its callbacks no matter what state the promise settles to as long as it is at the end of the chain. In this role it acts as a cleanup function.

The other methods of the jqXHR object are inherited from the browser's native XMLHttpRequest object, more of which later.

For example the previous load of "mydata.txt" can be written:

```
$.get("mydata.txt")
  .then(function(data){alert(data)});
```

Things get a little more interesting when you also define what is to happen if things go wrong and/or a clean up routine:

```
$.get("mydata.txt").then(
                    function (data) {
                      alert(data);
                    },
                    function () {
                      alert("error");
                    })
              .always(
               function () {
                alert("cleanup");
               });
```

Of course you don't have to define a handler for each of the events but this is the easiest way to do the job.

The parameters passed to the callbacks allow them to manipulate the data returned or examine the status of the call. The two functions used in the then` accept three parameters:

```
.then(function( data, textStatus, jqXHR ),
      function( jqXHR, textStatus, errorThrown )
```

and the always function uses either of the above parameter schemes depending on the success or failure of the call. That is:

```
.always(function( data, textStatus, jqXHR )
```

if successful or:

```
.always(function( jqXHR, textStatus, errorThrown )
```

if fail

**data** is the returned data.

**textStatus** is an object with a string value equal to one of:

- timeout
- error
- notmodified
- success
- parsererror

**errorThrown** is a string containing the message returned by the server. Obviously the range of possible responses depends on the server.

**jqXHR** is an object that can be used to find things out about the AJAX request. It is a superset of the browser's XMLHttpRequest object and has at least the following properties:

- ◆ responseText – the data returned
- ◆ response XML – the data if it is HTML or XML
- ◆ status – HTTP result code
- ◆ OK

and methods:

- ◆ getAllResponseHeaders() get all headers as a single string
- ◆ getResponseHeader("*header*") get the specified header as a string.

For example:

```
$.get("mydata.txt")
 .then(
     function (data,textStatus,jqXHR ) {
       alert(jqXHR.getResponseHeader("Host"));
     });
```

## Data Format

Exactly how the data is passed to the function depends on the MIME type of the response. This is usually set by the server as a header but jQuery will attempt to guess the right format if it isn't set.

Notice that in many cases the response from the server will be generated by a program – a PHP page say – but you can just specify the file of data you want transmitted and the server will load it and send it. When a program generates the data it is usual to make sure a header is properly set. When data is downloaded from a file the headers are usually left to the server.

More on headers and MIME in the following chapter.

If you know the format of the data you can specify it using a final parameter. The only complication is that you have to use place holders for the unused second and third parameters.

For example to tell jQuery that the file is XML you could use:

```
$.get("mydata.txt",null, null,"xml")
  .done(
    function (data) {
      alert(data);
    });
```

In this case data would be an XML root element of the tree constructed from the data transmitted. If the file doesn't contain XML data then you get an error condition.

The possibilities are:

- xml   -  XML root element
- json  - JSON object
- jsonp - JSONp object
- script - JavaScript file
- html  - String
- text   - String

If the data cannot be interpreted in the way you have set then an error is generated.

There are also some easy to use AJAX methods that will get JSON or Script data directly.

```
getJSON(url)
```

will retrieve a JSON object from the specified url and:

```
getScript(url)
```

will retrieve a script from the specified url.

Both work in the same way as the basic get and both return a Promise object.

If the data isn't in the correct format then an error occurs and the fail method of the Promise is called.

For example:

```
$.getJSON("myJSON.json")
  .then(
    function(data){
      alert(data.name);
    },
    function(){
      alert("error");
    });
```

assuming that the file myJSON has a name property set to some string e.g.

```
{
 "name": "Ian"
}
```

In the case of getScript the JavaScript is loaded and ready to run. It is also provided as a string as the first parameter to the done method.

For example:

```
$.getScript("myScript.js")
  .done(
    function(data){
      alert(data);
    },
    function(){
      alert("error");
    });
```

If myScript.js contains:

```
alert("hello remote script");
```

then you will see "hello remote script" before you see the alert listing the program. That is, the script is added before the done method gets to run.

A more reasonable example would be if myScript.js contains:

```
function doSomething(){
  alert("hello remote script");
};
```

Then it could be loaded and used something like:

```
$.getScript("myScript.js")
  .then(
    function(data){
      alert(data);
      doSomething();
    },
    function(){
      alert("error");
    });
```

The JavaScript is executed in the global context.

## Load

Finally there is one more variation on the basic get method – the load method. This performs a basic get, but it is slightly more integrated with the rest of jQuery in that it will set the HTML content of any matched elements.

However load is a strange method and doesn't fit in with the other AJAX methods. For example, it doesn't return a Promise object so you have to specify a success function. It does return a jQuery object so it can be chained.

For example:

```
$("body").load("myData.txt");
```

loads myData.txt and sets it as the body tag's HTML. Notice that if there are no matching elements the AJAX call isn't performed.

If you want to do something after the HTML has been loaded you need to supply a callback:

```
$("body").load("myData.txt",
            function(data){
              alert(data);
            });
```

Notice that the callback isn't just a success callback. It is a post processing callback.

The function that you supply is called once for each element in the selected set and this is set to each of the elements in turn. This allows you to scan through and modify the HTML that you have just loaded.

There is another strange extra behavior.

You can specify a portion of the returned HTML data to be used, i.e. a page fragment. If you follow the URL with a space and then a jQuery selector the selector is applied to the data before it is assigned to the matched elements.

That is, if you write:

```
  $("body").load("myData.txt #todaysData");
```

then the returned HTML is processed using $("#todaysData") and the result includes the matched element.

For example if myData.txt contains;

```
<div id="todaysData">
Sample Text
Sample Text
</div>
<div id="yesterdaysData">
Old Sample Text
Old Sample Text
</div>
```

then if you try:

```
$("body").load("myData.txt #todaysData",
            function(data){
              alert(data);
            });
```

You will see that the entire file has been returned in data, but only the first div has been inserted between <body> and </body>.

# Summary

- Before AJAX you could only load entire web pages. After AJAX you could load any file and process it to update the existing web page.

- jQuery provides a standardized and improved AJAX API.

- The simplest AJAX function is get which will return the contents of any file.

- Get returns an enhanced promise object which allows you to process the data.

- The promise that is returned also has the properties and methods of a normalized XMLHttpRequest object. This can be used to find out how the transaction was handled.

- You can also set a data format, or have one deduced from the data and this modifies the way jQuery treats the data.

- There are also specialized version of get – getJSON(url) will retrieve a JSON object from the specified url and getScript(url) will retrieve a script from the specified url.

- If all you want to do is add some HTML to the page then consider using the jQuery load function.

# Chapter 9

# AJAX Basics - Post

Now that we know all about how to get a file, it is time to post some data back to the server. In this chapter we look at both get and post as ways of sending data and see how to send form data under AJAX control.

As explained in the previous chapter, both get and post retrieve data and both can send data to the server, but we tend to use get to retrieve data and post to send data. Post was designed to send data to the server as suggested by its name but it proved important to have a way to send some data to the server even when using get and to achieve this we started to use the URL itself as a data transport.

Let's take a look at the simplest uses of post.

## Post

The jQuery post command is very easy to use but it can be difficult to get everything right on the client and on the server.

The basic command works exactly like get:

```
$.post(url)
```

which retrieves the file specified by the url and returns a jqXHR Promise object. You can specify a success callback as a parameter but as in the case of get it is easier to use the Promise object to define any callback.

For example:

```
$.post("myData.txt").then(
      function(data){
        alert(data)
      });
```

this simply asks the server for the file myData.txt stored in the same directory as the page making the request.

You can use the then, catch and always Promise methods as described in the previous chapter.

This all works but it is unusual to simply use a post request to retrieve the contents of a file. A `post` usually sends data to the server in the body of the request and jQuery lets you specify this data as the second parameter.

In principle you can send the data in any format you like as long as the server is able to deal with it. In practice jQuery provides automatic processing for a number of standard formats and it is easier to stick with these.

For example the simplest format to use is to send key value pairs which jQuery will extract from an object you supply. So for example if you want to send a first name, second name and an id number you could use:

```
var sendData={first:"ian",second:"elliot",id:27};

$.post("myData.txt",sendData).done(
                        function(data){
                          alert(data)
                        });
```

This sends the data to the server but of course the server just ignores it and sends the requested page back to the client.

To make use of the data there has to be a custom handler on the server to process the data. There are so many ways of doing this ranging from traditional CGI, JavaServlets, Node.js and so on.

For the sake of a concrete example we will use PHP to provide the server side processing.

The key idea is that the page that the `post` requests is best regarded as a program that processes the data and optionally returns a result to the client.

As long as you send data to a PHP page in key value pairs PHP will do you the favor of decoding them and will make them available as an associative array $_POST. This means that you have virtually no extra work to do on the server side to extract the data from a `post`.

You can also check that the request sent to the server was a `post` by testing the $_POST variable:

```
if($_POST){process data};
```

You also need to know that dots and spaces in the key will be converted to underscores e.g. a key like "I Programmer.info" is automatically converted to "I_Programmer_info".

You can handle the data sent by the previous example using a PHP file process.php something like;

```
<html>
 <head>
  <meta charset="UTF-8">
  <title></title>
 </head>
 <body>
  <?php
   echo( $_POST['first']);
  ?>
 </body>
</html>
```

which sends the first name back to the client within a web page.

PHP also automatically processes the value that you pass into either a string or an array according to its format. Notice that how and how much the data is preprocessed is a function of PHP not of the post request or AJAX transactions in general.

The general idea is that whatever method you use to process the data on the server it will usually provide you will some additional help and it is up to you to discover what it is and how to access the data.

So for example if we post the data:

```
var    sendData={first:"ian",
                 second:"elliot",
                 id:27.5,
                 array:[1,2,3]};
```

It could be processed in a PHP file something like:

```
echo(gettype($_POST["array"][1]));
```

which would return the string "2".

Notice that the array is a string array even though the values are numbers. If you want to work with numeric values then it is up to you to convert the data. This is because everything sent in an HTTP packet is text – there are no data types in the interaction.

Once again it is worth mentioning that it is the server side system you use that provides the data processing facilities and hence these are going to vary according to what you use.

If you are using PHP then it is worth looking up the filter_input function which can perform validation and conversion as well as sanitization of input. For example if you want the id field to be returned as an integer you could use:

```
 $id=filter_input(INPUT_POST,"id",FILTER_VALIDATE_INT);
```

This is by far the best way to work with any input data – post, get, cookie or server. This provision of functions that do the sort of tasks that you actually want to do is one of the reasons PHP is a good choice of server side languages. It may not be elegant but it is very practical.

So to summarize:

- Post sends data in the body of the request and retrieves data from the server but the file specified from the URL is expected to process the data sent.

- The data sent to the server can have any format but there are formats that are better supported than others in particular a string of key value pairs.

## Sending Data With Get

As mentioned in the previous chapter you can send data to the server with get almost as easily as with post but there are disadvantages.

When you send data to the server with get the data are encoded as the query string as part of the URL.

However, from the point of view of using jQuery there is no real difference between sending data using post or get. For example to send some data to be processed by process.php you would use:

```
$.get("process.php",sendData).then(
                        function(data){
                          alert(data)
                        });
```

which apart from the change from post to get is identical to the earlier program.

At the server side you simply have to change the $_POST to $_GET:

```
<?php  echo( $_GET['first']);
 echo(filter_input(INPUT_GET,"id",FILTER_VALIDATE_INT));
?>
```

This might well lull the beginner into a false sense of security because both the client and the server side systems are doing a lot of work to make things look this easy.

In particular jQuery does a lot of work for you and unpacks the key value pairs and URL encodes them. If you use the PHP instruction:

```
echo($_SERVER['REQUEST_URI']);
```

to send the URL back to the client for display then you will discover that it reads something like:

```
/process.php?first=ian&second=elliot&id=27&array%5B%5D=1&
                              array%5B%5D=2&array%5B%5D=3
```

The good news is that PHP automatically un-URLencodes the data for you and presents you with an array of key value pairs as in the case of post. That is, post and get send data to the server in two very different ways, but PHP and many other server side languages hide this difference from you as much as possible.

That is, when you use get all of the data is sent using the URL as a query string.

Different browsers limit the length of a URL in different ways but traditionally a limit of around 2000 characters has been suggested. However, why risk things not working when you can use a post instead.

If you want to manually URL encode some data use JavaScript's urlencode function or jQuery's param() function. The urlencode function will only code up a string and it is up to you to construct the full query string. The jQuery param() function will accept an array, object or jQuery object and do more of the work for you.

For example:

```
var q= $.param(sendData));
```

returns:

```
first=ian&second=elliot&id=27&array%5B%5D=1&array%5B%5D=2&
                              array%5B%5D=3
```

If you want to URL encode a form use jQuery's serialize method.

It is also worth knowing about the serializeArray method which will convert a form into an array of name value pairs. This is often useful if you need to do a lot of processing before sending the data.

The bottom line is that there is little reason to use a get to send a lot of complex data – you are better of with a post.

- If you are sending data to the server for processing use a post.
- If you are retrieving data from the server use a get.

The main use of data on `get` is in customizing the response. For example sending a page number to indicate which page of an article should be displayed is a reasonable use. Also keep in mind that the user can see the query string and is often tempted to try their hand at constructing their own or editing what you have provided.

## Where Is The Data?

When you use a `post` request things can get a little complicated with the interpretation of what is a URL and what is a local file system path. This is fairly straightforward and as long as you understand how URLs and file system paths work there should be no problem – however, having to use both at the same time can be confusing.

The program that processes the data will be loaded using a URL but often it has to save the data that has been sent using the local file system on the server and this can be confusing.

The path in an AJAX URL is always interpreted as starting at the website root. That is, you cannot request a file that is stored higher up in the local file system.

As far as the AJAX URL is concerned the website root directory is its root directory.

That is in a URL:

- An absolute path always starts at the website root.
- A relative path starts at the folder that the page making the request is stored in.

That is, if your website root is:

`/var/www/`

and the home page is:

`myserver.com/index.html`

then an absolute path in a `get` performed within the home page such as:

`/mydirectory/mydata.txt`

will get the same file as a relative path mydirectory/mydata.txt, i.e. the file:

`/var/www/mydirectory/mydata.txt`

Now we come to the slight complication.

Suppose the PHP program is to save the data and it is supplied a path to a folder to save the data to.

For example:

```
var sendData={dir:"mydirectory/", myData:"some data"};

$.post("process.php",sendData).then(
                                function(data){
                                  console.log(data);
                                });
```

The following PHP program can get the directory and the data and save the data as requested:

```
<?php
 $dir=$_POST["dir"];
 $data=$_POST["myData"];
 $result= file_put_contents($dir."myFile", $data);
 echo($result);
?>
```

The file myFile will be stored in the mydirectory folder in the folder that the page was served from. If we assume that the page was served from the site root then the folder, in terms of the local file system, is:

```
var/www/mydirectory/
```

In other words, it is the same directory that a relative URL of the form mydirectory/ would have referred to.

Now consider how to specify an absolute path to mydirectory – perhaps because you want to store the file in the same folder no matter where the page that makes the AJAX call was served from. By analogy with a URL which always takes a path as relative to the website root you might try:

```
var    sendData={dir:"/mydirectory/",myData:"some data"};
```

Now the program doesn't work unless there is a mydirectory folder in the root of the local file system that the PHP page has permissions to write to.

That is /mydirectory/ in this case is a reference to mydirectory in the root of the local file system not in the website root.

This is perfectly reasonable as the PHP instruction is a file system command and hence it works with the usual rules of the local file system – absolute paths are from the file system root, and relative paths are relative to the directory that the program is run from. However, the change from relative to absolute can still be confusing in going from a URL to a local file system path.

You can make this situation worse or better depending on your point of view by writing your server side programs to append the web directory's path. That is append /var/www to every path that the AJAX call provides. This allows the URL to refer to the same file as the file system path, but if the user or the client side program doesn't know this then things still go wrong.

# AJAX and Forms

Get and post were used to send data to the server and get a response long before AJAX was invented. HTML forms use either get or post to send the data that the user enters to the server. This is where it all started, but today you can opt to handle forms yourself via AJAX.

First a quick refresher on HTML forms.

You create a form using the form tag, which contains a set of input elements.

For example:

```
<form action="process.php" method="post">
 First name:<br>
 <input type="text" name="first" value="Enter Data">
 <br>
 Last name:<br>
 <input type="text" name="last" value="Enter Data">
 <br><br>
 <input type="submit" value="Submit">
</form>
```

The user can now enter data, first name, last name and when they click the submit button the data is sent to the server. The request method used is set by method, which can be post or get. The data in the form are encoded as key value pairs. The key is the name of each input element and the value is its value.

How the key value pairs are encoded depends on the method  - they are coded as the query string part of the URL if is is get, and within the request body for a post. The program that is loaded by the server is specified by the action attribute.

So in this case when the user clicks the submit button the data in first and last is coded up as:

```
first:firstname,last:lastname
```

and sent to process.php.

If the method had been set to get, i.e. method="get", then the data would have been coded as part of the URL, something like:

```
http://host/process.php?first=Enter+Data&last=Enter+Data
```

A PHP program to process the form data would be something like:

```
<?php
 $first=$_POST["first"];
 $last=$_POST["last"];
 echo($first.$last);
?>
```

and this just sends the first and last name back to the client as the response.

If this sounds a lot like the get and post you have been working with as part of AJAX then you are correct. This is where the AJAX protocol for data transfer originated – AJAX just took over what forms had been doing for ages.

So what exactly is the difference?

The difference is that with a form-based data submission the file specified as the action is returned to the client as an HTML page and it replaces the page that made the request.

If you send the form data using AJAX then the AJAX done method receives the response and can do with it what it likes. The page that makes the request is not replaced by the response.

For example, let's suppose we want to send the same form data to the server using AJAX.

First we have to do something about the submit button because when the user clicks it the client starts the get or post without giving you a chance to customize anything. There are many ways of activating the AJAX operation and the simplest is just to use a standard button with a suitable onClick event handler. The big problem is that clients often treat the Enter key as a signal to submit the form.

The best way of intercepting the submit button is to attach an event handler of our own. This is particularly easy using jQuery and the submit method. The only change we have to make to the form is to give the form tag an id:

```
<form id="myForm" action="process.php" method="post">
```

Now we can add a submit event handler:

```
$("#myForm").submit(
             function(event){
               alert("submit");
             })
```

When the user clicks the submit button our event handler is called but the post to the server still occurs because the event propagates to the client's built-in event handler.

To stop the propagation we could return false or use the preventDefault method:

```
$("#myForm").submit(
             function(event){
               event.preventDefault();
             })
```

With this change the user can click the submit button or perform any action that causes the form to be submitted and the event handler will be called and the form will not be submitted. It is better to use preventDefault because it only stops the default event handler being called. Returning false stops the event completely.

Now we have control of the submit process all we have to do is arrange for the form's data to be sent to the server, but first we have to encode it appropriately because this is no longer done for us. The simplest way to do this is to use the jQuery serialize data method:

```
var sendData=$(this).serialize();
```

We use this in the submit event handler because it is set to the element that originated the event.

Putting all this together gives:

```
$("#myForm").submit(
            function(event){
              event.preventDefault();
              var sendData=$(this).serialize();
              $.post("process.php", sendData)
                      .done(
                         function (data) {
                           console.log(data);
                         });
            });
```

Notice that now the data returned by the server doesn't replace the current page and in this case it is simply printed to the console.

A get works in exactly the same way and the server side code doesn't need to be modified from its basic form handling to cope with data sent by AJAX rather than the default submit.

The only difference is that the data returned doesn't replace the page.

What advantage does this have?

The answer to this question ranges from something sophisticated, e.g. because you are writing a single page application, to the fairly obvious, e.g. because you don't want the page context to change because of a form submit.

For example, you could check that the form contains valid data before posting it to the server, and if not the form wouldn't be cleared by the page that overwrites it. In other words, the user's context, i.e. any data they may have entered, remains unaltered by the submit.

It is also the case that submitting data using AJAX means that the user isn't subjected to the loading of a new page.

# Summary

- The jQuery command $.post(url) sends data to the url specified. The url usually corresponds to a program that will process the data but it also sends a new HTML page back to the client.

- A post usually sends data to the server in the body of the request and jQuery lets you specify this data as the second parameter.

- The simplest format to use is to send key value pairs which jQuery will extract from an object you supply.

- The server side system you use provides the data processing facilities and hence these are going to vary according to what you use.

- When you send data to the server with get the data are encoded as the query string as part of the URL.

- If you want to manually URL encode some data use JavaScript's urlencode function or jQuery's param() function.

- In a form-based data submission the file specified as the action is returned to the client as an HTML page and it replaces the page that made the request.

- If you send the form data using AJAX then the AJAX done method receives the response and can do with it what it likes. The page that makes the request is not replaced by the response.

# Chapter 10

# Sending Data To The Server

So far in our exploration of jQuery we have used the "shorthand" AJAX methods. These are all implemented as calls to the full jQuery `ajax` method and if you want to do anything slightly out of the ordinary then you need to make use of it directly. In this chapter we look at controlling the request and sending data to the server

## Raw AJAX method

The raw or low level AJAX method is very easy to specify. You can call it either using:

```
$.ajax(url,options);
```

or just as

```
$.ajax(options);
```

with the url specified as part of the options object.

All of the complexities of using it are hidden in the options object. This is a set of key value pairs that you use to specify how the AJAX request should be performed.

Notice that the only difference between the two forms of using the ajax method is that if you don't specify the url as the first parameter it has to be specified in the options object.

The simplest post request using the ajax method is something like:

```
var options={};
options.url="process.php";
options.method="post";
options.data={first:"ian",last:"elliot",id:27};

$.ajax(options).then(
                function(data){
                  alert(data);
                });
```

That is, the url property sets the request url, the method sets the method to post in this case, and the data property is the data sent to the server.

This is all there is the ajax method and all that remains to do is investigate the various options you can set.

139

Instead of dealing with the options in alphabetical order, which is what the documentation does, it is more useful to look at them in groups according to what they are concerned with.

## Controlling the request

There are a set of options that modify the very basic nature of the AJAX request. Instead of just presenting them as an alphabetic list, it is worth dealing with them in logical groups.

You need to read the first section on controlling the basic HTTP call.

## Basic HTTP call

There are a set of options that control the basic nature of the HTTP request being made and how it is handled.

**It is important that you read the section on ifModified and cache.**

- **url**
  sets the url of the request. For example:
  options.url="process.php";
- **method** or **type**
  method sets the type of request, and you can use type as an alias for method. You can set it to GET, POST. PUT or HEAD. Its default is GET. For example:
  options.method="post";
- **async**
  you can force a request to be handled in a synchronous way. If you do this then your JavaScript will wait for the request to complete and the UI will freeze. The default setting is true and this is how you generally should leave it. There are very few, if any, uses of synchronous AJAX requests and jsonp in particular doesn't support it.
- **ifModified** and **cache**
  Setting ifModified to true will cause the AJAX request to fail if the browser detects that the resource hasn't changed since it was last requested. Setting cache to false forces get and put to retrieve the resource even if it is available in the cache.
  ifModified and cache control whether a resource is retrieved over the network or not and this is a topic which deserves separate treatment.

◆ **timeout**
Sets the timeout for the request in milliseconds. The timing starts from the attempt to make the request so it can include time spent queuing for the client to deal with it. What this means is that you might have to factor in additional time over and above the response time of the server.

## Only getting new data

Sooner or later you will fall foul of cached results.

The standard waste of time is that you send some data to the server using post and retrieve it using get. The first time you do this it seems to work but later on any changes you make to the data aren't reflected in the data you get back from get.

The reason for this is that by default post doesn't cache data but get does.

Put simply, if you request the same URL more than once using get then the browser will cache the first request and use this for the data for all subsequent requests.

One possible solution is to use a different URL for all get operations by adding something unique to the end of the query string, but it is simpler to set cache to false and get jQuery to do the job for you. If cache is set to false then jQuery will add a query string "_=timestamp" to get and put requests - of course post never uses cached data.

For example:

```
options.cache=false;
```

Related to caching is ifModified. If this is set to true then the AJAX call only works if the response has changed since the last request. It basically checks the time in the Last-Modified header to the time of the last request. Notice that this first retrieves just the headers of the HTTP request needed for the resource and so this can save downloading something that hasn't changed. However, making this work consistently is a matter of dealing with different browser and server behavior.

So to make sure you get the latest version of the data and only fetch the data if it has been updated since the last fetch you would use:

```
var options={};
options.url="process.php";
options.method="get";
options.cache=false;
options.ifModified=true;
$.ajax(options).then(
                function(data){
                  alert(data);
                });
```

If the file hasn't been updated since the last request then the `then` method will be called but `data` will be undefined.

Only use ifModified if the resource requested is big because trying to save downloads usually causes trouble for some browsers and it also depends on the headers that the server includes.

For example if you try:

```
var options={};
options.url="mydata.txt";
options.method="get";
options.cache=false;
options.ifModified=true;

$.ajax(options).then(
                function(data){
                  console.log(data);
                });

window.setTimeout(
            function(){
              $.ajax(options).then(
                                function(data){
                                  console.log(data);
                                })
            },5000);
```

then what you will see depends mostly on the server. Most servers will send a Last-Modified header and the second AJAX request for the static file will fail because it hasn't been modified in the 5 second interval. In this case `then` will still be called but you will see `undefined` displayed i.e. the data isn't retrieved.

However, if you try it with say the built in PHP server, you will find that you get the static file twice because it doesn't send the header and so each AJAX request transfers the file.

Notice that setting cache=true doesn't change the result, the request still usually fails if the Last-Modified header indicates that there has been no change to the file. The problem is that some older browsers load the data from the cache even if the data hasn't changed.

There are many other problems, far too many to deal with in this chapter, in trying to avoid resources being reloaded unnecessarily. For example an AJAX request will generally be remade after a page load even if the resource is still in the cache.

## Data sent to the server

As we already know, both `get` and `post` send data to the server and receive data from the server. There are options to control the data in both directions – let's look at the "to the server" direction first and look at the client direction in the next chapter.

When you make an AJAX request you can specify the following options to control the data sent to the server:

- **data**
  The data sent to the server – it can be a general Object, String or Array.
  If it is a string it has to be in query string format.
  If it is an object or an array it has to be convertible into query string format. That is, the object or array has to be regarded as key value pairs.
  For a `get` request it is added to the URL as a query string, and for a `post` request it is sent in the body of the request.

- **ContentType**
  This option sets the value of the Content-Type header sent with the request. This informs the server how the content of should be interpreted. Notice that this only works with a `post` (or a put) request as the content type of a `get` is always the default application/x-www-form-urlencoded; charset=UTF-8. Notice also that you cannot change the character encoding as it is part of the AJAX standard. Sending a header doesn't mean that the server will do anything very different - see later for more information.

- **Traditional**
  By default this is false and it enables recursive encoding of complex data. Set to true to fall back to the original non-recursive scheme.

- **ProcessData**
  If set to false it stops jQuery processing any of the data. In other words if processData is false jQuery simply sends whatever you specify as data in an AJAX request without any attempt to modify it by encoding as a query string.  - this is a rarely used but useful facility and is described in more detail in the next section.

## Encoding the sent data

The only real issue with the data sent to the server is how it is coded into a query string.

The default content type for get, post and put is application/x-www-form-urlencoded which means that the data is sent as a stream of key value pairs using URL encoding, and the UTF-8 character encoding. We will return to character encoding in a later chapter.

You can send data in other formats but only using post or put – more about how to do this later.

In most cases form-urlencoded data is the one to stick with, because it is more or less automatic at both the client and the server end of the request. If you are deriving data from a form then it will be automatically encoded for you. If you get the data from some other source then it has to be encoded.

This task is performed by the param() method.

If the data is a string then it is assumed to be in the correct format for a query string. For example:

```
options.data="first=ian&last=elliot";
```

If the data is an object then it will be converted to the query string by the param() method:

```
options.data={first:"ian",last:"elliot"};
```

results in the same query string as given earlier.

If the data is an array then it has to be an array of key value objects, each object giving the name of the key and the value. For example, to code the data used in the previous examples:

```
options.data=[
            {name:"first",value:"ian"},
            {name:"last",value:"elliot"}
          ]
```

Notice that the array has one element for each of the key value pairs. You can see that this is a longer way of specifying the data but sometimes it is more convenient.

As well as converting the data to a query string format, also notice that the usual URL encoding is performed to represent characters that are not in the ASCII character set. So for example a space is replaced by %20, " by %22, and so on. If you decide to send the query string as a string that you construct yourself you need to make sure that it is URL encoded.

So far so simple.

However, jQuery and many server frameworks can cope with a much more complicated data structure than a simple "flat" set of key value pairs. That is, you can code into a query string something more complex. The idea is that the encoding method is called recursively to encode any value that might itself be a more complex data structure.

For example consider:

```
var cdata={
          array:[1,2,3],
          object:{first:"ian",last:"elliot"}
          }
```

This would be coded as:

```
array%5B%5D=1&array%5B%5D=2&array%5B%5D=
3&object%5Bfirst%5D=ian&object%5Blast%5D=elliot
```

You could send this to the server and it would be received as a perfectly valid query string, but reconstructing what it represents is a matter for the software you use on the server. For example in PHP reconstruction is simple:

```
$array=$_POST["array"];
$object=$_POST["object"];
```

After this $array is indeed an array and you could access $array[0] to retrieve 1 and so on. The variable $object is a PHP associative array and you can access the object fields using expressions like $object["first"].

Notice that this only works because PHP supports recursive query strings.

If you don't want this, recursive coding simply sets the option `traditional` to true.

Recursive encoding seems attractive but the big problem with it is that there is no agreed standard. It works with PHP and Ruby, but other languages and frameworks might not support it. This is fine when you control both the client and the server side of the interaction but it does make your code less portable.

A better alternative is to use JSON to code the data and make a JSON AJAX request.

## General objects as data – processData

Finally we come to the strange and misunderstood processData.

If you set this to false then jQuery will not process whatever you store in the data option. That is, no conversion to string and no encodings are performed.

What possible purpose could this serve?

It first it seems that the only data you could send with processData set to false is string data because this is what the AJAX request requires – the AJAX request can only send formatted string data. As string data is never processed by jQuery AJAX there seems to be little point in setting processData to false when sending it.

This of course forgets the simple fact that every JavaScript object has a string value as determined by its toString method.

When you set data to a general object other than a string with processData set to true, jQuery attempts to process the object to create a query string.

When you set data to a general object other than a string with processData set to false, jQuery doesn't process the object. The object is passed to the AJAX call exactly as it is and used as if it was a String. This by default calls the toString method and sends the result to the server as the data in the AJAX request.

In this way any object can be the data in an AJAX request as long as it returns a sensible string value from toString.

For example, suppose you define an object:

```
myObject={}
myObject.toString= function(){
               return "first=ian&last=elliot"
            };
```

You can see that the string value of myObject is a valid query string correctly encoded. Now if you set the relevant part options to:

```
options.data=myObject;
options.processData=false;
```

and send the AJAX request, myObject will not be processed to a string, but when the AJAX call is made, its toString method will be called and the query string will be sent as data.

Using this technique you can extend the range of objects that can be sent via AJAX to the server. Simply define your custom object, define its toString method to serialize the object or the data it represents, and use it with processData set to false.

There are already some objects in JavaScript that can be sent in this way because they have correct serializations defined as their toString methods. Perhaps the best known is the FormData object which can be used to build up key value pairs either in code or from an HTML form.

# Other content types

So far we have only considered sending form-urlencoded data because this is the easiest thing to do and it is versatile. However, there are times when you might want to send data in other formats to the server – usually either XML or JSON but custom formats are possible. This is easy to do at the client end, the problems usually arise at the server end because the data isn't automatically processed like form-urlencoded data.

Notice that sending data in other formats only makes sense for `post` and `put` requests. The reason is that for `get` the data is coded as part of the URL, the query string, and for this to work it has to be in the form-urlencoded format. All you have to do to send data in a different format is to change the Content-Type header sent to the server.

## XML

For example, to send XML data you could use:

```
options.contentType="text/xml";
```

This changes the default Content-Type header from:

```
Content-Type: application/x-www-form-urlencoded
```

to:

```
Content-Type: text/xml
```

The header is sent to the server with the request, but nothing else changes at the client end of the request. That is, if you provide the data as anything other than a `string`, jQuery will process it to produce form-urlencoded data. This probably isn't what you want and so it makes sense to turn off processing using:

```
options.processData=false;
```

However, in most cases the data to be sent will be in a string and jQuery doesn't bother making an attempt to convert it. That is no matter what the Content-Type header is jQuery just sends the `string` as the data payload in the body of the request. The string is converted to a stream of bytes in UTF-8 code and in nearly all cases the server side will convert the UTF-8 bytes into a string that is native to the framework. That is, on the server side whatever data is sent as a `string` is received as a string.

For example, suppose we want to send the following XML stored in a `string` to the server:

```
cdata="\<\?xml version=\"1.0\" \?\>";
cdata+="<Books>";
cdata+="<Title>Life of Pi</Title>";
cdata+="<Author>Yann Martel</Author >";
cdata+="</Books>";
```

Notice the need to escape some of the characters in the first string.

This can be sent to the server using:

```
var options={};
options.url="process.php";
options.method="post";
options.data=cdata;
options.contentType="text/xml";

$.ajax(options).then(
                  function(data){
                    console.log(data);
                  });
```

This much is easy but how to handle the data on the server side is more tricky and depends on what is being used to process it. The key fact is that at the very least you can expect the string to be recoverable from the raw AJAX data.

In PHP for example you can read the string:

```
$xml = file_get_contents('php://input');
echo($xml);
```

and the string:

```
<?xml version="1.0" ?><Books><Title>Life of Pi</Title><Author>Yann Martel</Author ></Books>
```

will be inserted into the page.

Of course PHP has facilities for working with XML so you could convert the string into an XMLelement:

```
$xml = file_get_contents('php://input');
$xmlData = simplexml_load_string($xml);
echo($xmlData->Title);
```

The $xmlData object has properties corresponding to the XML tags.

## JSON

Working with JSON is arguably easier because both JavaScript and PHP have good support for it.

First you need to convert your JSON to a string:

```
cdata=JSON.stringify({first:"ian",last:"elliot"});
```

Now you can send it in the same way as the XML was sent by changing the ContentType header:

```
var options={};
options.url="process.php";
options.method="post";
options.data=cdata;
options.contentType="application/json";
$.ajax(options).then(
                function(data){
                   console.log(data);
                });
```

As before the data is sent unmodified and the server receives it in the usual way. In PHP you have to process the received string to a suitable object.

For example:

```
$json = json_decode(file_get_contents('php://input'));
echo($json->first);
```

sends "Ian" back to the client.

## Other HTTP Methods

jQuery only provides short cut functions for get and post. The reason is that these two are mostly what you want to use but there are other HTTP methods. HTTP/1.0 defined GET, POST and HEAD. We have covered GET and POST in detail.

HEAD operates exactly like GET but it only returns the response headers i.e. there is no response body. You can use this to find out the status of the web page without having to download all its content. For example:

```
$.ajax(
        { url: "webpage.htm",
          type: "HEAD" }
      ).then(
          function(data, textStatus, jqXHR){
            alert(jqXHR.getAllResponseHeaders());
          },
          function(error){
            alert("error");
          });
```

If you try this out using a development server such as the one provided with NetBeans or the PHP server, you will discover it doesn't work. Simple development servers usually don't support anything other than GET and POST. When you go beyond GET, POST and HEAD then most production servers have to be configured to respond to them.

HTTP/1.1 introduced OPTIONS, PUT, DELETE, TRACE and CONNECT. Of these only PUT and DELETE are often used.

PUT is like a POST, but the URL provided isn't the program you want to process the data, it is the URL you would like the data to be stored under. If the file exists then the data is used to update it and if it doesn't the server should create it. Obviously you can't simply let any client create or overwrite files on the server and different servers have different ways of controlling PUT. For example the Apache server lets you specify a program that is called to handle the request. You can think of this as POST but with a fixed program to do the data processing. If you are playing by the rules then you should take the data that has been sent and save it under the file name specified by the URL. Here is a PHP program that does exactly this:

```
$putdata = fopen("php://input", "r");
$fp = fopen("puttemp.ext", "w");
while ($data = fread($putdata, 1024))
                        fwrite($fp, $data);
fclose($fp);
fclose($putdata);
```

The only thing you need to know to understand this program is that PUT raw data comes in from php://input. The PUT data is stored in a file called puttemp so that it can be validated before being renamed to whatever the user specified. You also need to add:

```
Script PUT pathToScript
```

to the configuration file inside a <Directory> block.

The important thing to realize is that PUT only works if the server is set up to handle it, and there is nothing to say that the server has to play by your expectations. A server should save or update the resource indicated by the URL and the data, but it doesn't have to.

To use jQuery to send a PUT you would use something like:

```
$.ajax({
        url: url,
        type: 'PUT',
        data: data,
        contentType: type
        }).then(success,fail);
```

Notice that a PUT doesn't return any data.

DELETE is supposed to delete the file at the specified URL, but of course no server would do this as a default action. As for PUT, Apache requires a fixed script to be used. So for example if you wanted to enable PUT and DELETE on the entire website (not a good idea) then you would use:

```
<Location />
  Script PUT /handler1.php
  Script DELETE /handler2.php
</Location>
```

In each case you would have to program the handler to check the validity of what was about to happen. In most cases the DELETE handler would delete the specified file, but as for PUT this is not enforced. You can do whatever you want in the handlers.

The final three, TRACE, OPTIONS and CONNECT are rarely encountered. TRACE echos the request back to the client for testing and debugging purposes. OPTIONS returns the methods that the server supports for that URL. Finally CONNECT requests a connection to a TCP/IP tunnel. All of these require web server configuration to enable them.

# Summary

- The main AJAX method is $.ajax(url,options); or $.ajax(options); with the url included as one of the options.

- There are a set of options that control the basic nature of the HTTP request being made and how it is handled.

- The ifModified and cache options are vital if you want to see the latest data.

- A post is never cached.

- The default content type for `get`, `post` and `put` is application/x-www-form-urlencoded which means that the data is sent as a stream of key value pairs using URL encoding and the UTF-8 character encoding.

- In most cases form-urlencoded data is the best supported data format.

- If you are deriving data from a form then it will be automatically encoded for you. If you get the data from some other source then it has to be encoded by the param() method.

- jQuery and many server frameworks support more complex data types including arrays and objects, but still using form-urlencoding.

- You can also use general objects as data sources as long as you define the toString method to serialize the data.

- You can also send xml and json to the server but you will have arrange for some processing to convert to a String and then back again to the format.

- HTTP/1.0 defined GET, POST and HEAD and HTTP/1.1 introduced OPTIONS, PUT, DELETE, TRACE and CONNECT. Of these only GET, POST and HEAD are frequently used. PUT and DELETE need server configuration to enable them.

# Chapter 11
## Sending Data To The Client

An AJAX request is a two-way interaction. Some data is sent to the server and the server sends some data back to the client. In this chapter we look at the problems of sending data to the client from the server using the low level AJAX method.

All HTTP requests return data from the server. The `get` and the `post` methods are designed originally to return an HTML page from the server for the client to display. Of course the whole point of using AJAX is that the "page" that the server returns doesn't have to be displayed and can be processed as general data in any way that the client sees fit. The only problem is that while there are a lot of built in data transformations and types that are designed to be useful and make life easier for you, they can sometimes get between you and the data.

## Response data options

There are a set of options that modify the way that data received from the server is processed before being returned to your function.

First recall that there is no option that accepts data from the server like the one that specifies data to be transmitted to the server. As the data sent from the server is received asynchronously, the return data is passed into a callback as a parameter.

The two key parameters that control, or rather try to control, the server's response are `dataType` and `accepts`. While these seem simple enough when you first encounter them, they are not as simple as they initially appear. In fact they work together in a way that really isn't well explained in the documentation.

- ◆ **Accepts**
  the type of data the client wants back from the server as indicated in the Accept request header.
- ◆ **DataType**
  the type of data the client expects back from the server – a selection of xml, html, script, json, jsonp or text.

You can immediately see that these two options seem to control the same thing – the type of the data returned by the server. In fact they work together on the problem.

If you don't set a dataType then jQuery sends a default accept header:

```
Accept:*/*
```

which means "send me anything".

When the data arrives from the server jQuery attempts to work out what it is, based on the MIME type specified in the Content-Type header returned by the server.

If you set a `dataType` and don't set `accepts` then jQuery will send a suitable Accept header. For example if you set `dataType` to html using:

```
options.dataType="html";
```

then the Accept header changes to:

```
Accept: text/html, */*; q=0.01
```

The q parameter indicates the preference for the */* type. i.e. "you can send me anything other than html but I really don't like it". Without the q or relative quality parameter defaults to 1 and the server might send nothing at all.

If you want some other form of the Accept header you can make use of the `accepts` option to partially override the default. You can only partially override the default because no matter what you specify you always get "*/*;q=0.01" appended to the end.

The `accepts` option has to be set to an object of key value pairs. The keys are the datatypes and the values are the replacement data types to put into the Accept header.

For example:

```
options.accepts={html:"text/html;q=0.9",
                 xml: "application/xml;q=0.1"};
```

sets the header to:

```
Accept: text/html;q=0.9, */*; q=0.01
```

if the `dataType` is set to "html".

Notice that if the `dataType` is set to a space-separated set of types, only the first type changes the Accept header.

For example:

```
dataType="html xml";
```

will only set the Accept header using the html entry in `accepts`.

That is the header will be:

```
Accept: textl;q=0.9, */*; q=0.01
```

## The dataType and the Server

The idea of setting the `dataType` that you expect or require depending on how you look at it is a bit strange. In most HTTP, requests that `dataType` or MIME type should be exact is determined by the file retrieved by the server. An html file has a MIME type of text/html, if you request a png file then the type is image/png. The data is retrieved by the server and the appropriate headers are generated to give the client the information it needs to identify and in some cases process the data.

The question that we have to answer is, how does a server side program, a PHP program for example, generate a response with a specific type?

The key idea is that the program has to generate the appropriate headers for the type of data it is sending to the client.

For example, suppose we want to send some xml data to the client, then the PHP program has to send a Content-Type header using the header instruction. The only difficulty with this is that the header instruction has to be the very first in the program because it has to be before the server has started to generate its default headers. In a PHP program any blank lines are sent to the client as part of an HTML page so the header instruction really does have to be at the very start of the file. To send some XML data you would use something like:

```php
<?php
header("Content-Type: application/xml");

$cdata='<?xml version="1.0" encoding="UTF-8"?>';
$cdata.="<Books>";
$cdata.="<Title>Life of Pi</Title>";
$cdata.="<Author>Yann Martel</Author >";
$cdata.="</Books>";
echo($cdata);
?>
```

and the <?php tag has to be the first in the file.

The jQuery to get this data can be something like:

```
var options={};
options.url="process.php";
options.method="post";
options.dataType="xml";

$.ajax(options).then(
                function(data){
                  console.log(data);
                });
```

Setting the dataType to xml and/or setting accept to send a custom header to the server really doesn't make a lot of difference as the MIME type sent by the server is enough to make jQuery process the data returned as XML. In fact if you do set the dataType option to "xml" then the server doesn't need to send the correct MIME type in the header and things work in the same way.

The key point is that in this case jQuery takes the raw data sent by the server and converts it into an XML object. That is, in the callback data is no longer a string but an XML object created by calling jQuery.parseXML on the raw data. You can make use of this method to convert your own valid XML strings into an XML object. To work with the XML object you need to look its details up in the XML DOM documentation.

For example, to get the textnode corresponding to Title you would have to use:

```
$.ajax(options).then(
                function(data){
                  var nodelist=data.getElementsByTagName('Title');
                  var textnode=nodelist[0].childNodes[0];
                  console.log(textnode.nodeValue);
                });
```

Notice the XML DOM and node object is provided by the browser and not by jQuery. The jQuery.parseXML makes use of the browser's built in XML facilities.

Working with an XML DOM object isn't as easy as working with jQuery but you can convert it to a jQuery object. For example:

```
$.ajax(options).then(
                function(data){
                  var xml=$(data);
                  console.log(xml.find("Title").text());
                  console.log(xml.find("Author").text());
                });
```

# Other types of data

If you want to receive other types of data you have to go through the same basic steps.

1. Either get the server to set the correct Content-Type header and/or set the `dataType` option. Preferably do both.

2. Set a custom Require header using the `requires` property if needed.

3. Discover how jQuery returns the data for the specified data type:

   | | |
   |---|---|
   | **xml** | an XML DOM object |
   | **html** | a string |
   | **script** | a string but browser also runs the JavaScript |
   | **json** | a JSON object |
   | **text** | a String |
   | **jsonp** | the browser loads and runs the script. |

# Examples in PHP and JavaScript

Let's have a simple example of each one, apart from jsonp, in addition to XML in PHP and JavaScript. The reason jsonp is omitted is that as it is more complicated than the rest, it deserves a section all to itself, see the next chapter.

### Html

In theory you don't need to send an explicit header for HTML because this is the default for a PHP page:

```php
<?php
header("Content-Type:text/html;charset=UTF-8");
$cdata='<div id="todaysData">Sample Text<br/></div>';
echo($cdata);
?>
```

The client gets the data as a String but of course you can use jQuery to convert it to a jQuery object and insert it into the DOM after processing:

```javascript
var options={};
options.url="process.php";
options.method="post";
options.dataType="html";
$.ajax(options).then(
                function(data){
                  console.log(data);
                  $("body").append(data);
                });
```

## Script

Loading a script is simple, but you have to keep in mind that the browser will add the script to the JavaScript environment. For example, the following PHP program will supply a simple script:

```php
<?php
header("Content-Type:application/javascript;charset=UTF-8");
$cdata='alert("hello remote script");
        function doSomething(){alert("hello remote script");
        return 10;};';
echo($cdata);
?>
```

The client program is:

```javascript
var options={};
options.url="process.php";
options.method="post";
$.ajax(options).then(
                function(data){
                  console.log(data);
                  doSomething();
                });
```

Notice that when you run the client, the alert appears at once and you can call the doSomething function – the code has been added to the JavaScript.

There is a subtlety about the script data type. If you make a script request to the same domain as the page was served from then a standard AJAX call is made and the text that is received is processed by a function which is equivalent to:

```javascript
function(text){
 jQuery.globalEval(text);
 return text;
}
```

This is in fact a converter function, see later, which converts text to script.

However, if the request is to a domain other than the page that was loaded then a completely different method of downloading the script is used as the standard AJAX transport doesn't allow for cross domain requests. See the next chapter for details.

## Json

The only complication with JSON is that web servers often don't set the Content-Type header correctly when you get or post a .json file. This means that you have to set the dataType to json or use getJSON to convert the data to a JavaScript object.

If you are using PHP or some dynamic generator of JSON then you can ensure that that the header is set correctly:

```php
<?php
header("Content-Type:application/json;charset=UTF-8");
$cdata='{"first": "Ian","last":"Elliot"}';
echo($cdata);
?>
```

The client will now correctly deal with the JSON it receives and will convert the raw String data into a JavaScript object:

```javascript
var options={};
options.url="process.php";
options.method="post";
$.ajax(options).then(
                function(data){
                   console.log(data);
                });
```

With the correct header sent there is no need to set `dataType` but it doesn't hurt to:

```javascript
options.dataType="json";
```

The data that is returned is a JavaScript object with properties `first` and `last`.

## Text

There almost isn't anything to say about text – the server sends a string and the client receives a string.

The PHP is:

```php
<?php
header("Content-Type:text/plain;charset=UTF-8");
$cdata="This is a string";
echo($cdata);
?>
```

Notice that you can use other sub-types for more structured data such as text/csv and so on. It is up to you, however, to provide the additional processing as jQuery will just return the data as a string:

```javascript
var options={};
options.url="process.php";
options.method="post";
$.ajax(options).then(
                function(data){
                   console.log(data);
                });
```

The data is displayed as a simple string. There are a few more things to say about sending string data concerning character encoding but this is discussed in a more general setting later.

# Custom content headers

In most cases the options that jQuery provides for data handling are sufficient. If you need to send some custom data then the simplest thing to do is send it as String, encoded if necessary, and then write your own functions to code it.

However, jQuery does provide some facilities to help you process custom data.

## MimeType

If you know that the data that the server is sending you is one of the standard types you can override any Content-Type headers that specify a different type. This can also be useful when you want to treat JSON as Text say. That is if the server sends you:

```
<?php
header("Content-Type:application/json;charset=UTF-8");
$cdata='{"first": "Ian","last":"Elliot"}';
echo($cdata);
?>
```

Then by default jQuery will construct a JavaScript object for you with the first and last properties. If you set:

```
options.mimeType="text/plain";
```

then jQuery will treat the data as if it was plain text. Notice that in this case there is no difference between setting mimeType or dataType to text. In general, however, mimeType replaces the Content-Type header and this could affect any further processing. You can also set it to values that are outside of the range of dataType.

Now we come to a complicated part of using jQuery AJAX – converters. If you don't want to know how jQuery creates different types of data or if you don't want to implement your own data types then you don't need to know about type converters.

# Type Converters

When you specify one of the data types in `dataType` jQuery invokes a converter. A converter is a function that takes one data type and turns it into another. At its simplest you can specify a single built-in data type and jQuery will call a single converter function. For example when you do a request for a script data type to the same domain, jQuery downloads the script using the standard AJAX request as text and then automatically invokes the converter function:

```
function(text){
 jQuery.globalEval(text);
 return text;
}
```

i.e. a text to script converter.

If you want to do something more complex, you can actually specify a set of data types and jQuery will attempt to perform each data conversion in turn. For example:

```
options.dataType="json text xml";
```

causes jQuery to first convert to json, then to text and then to xml. This isn't particularly realistic but it conveys the principle.

The next piece of information you need to know is that all AJAX requests return text to the client and it is jQuery that does the conversion to whatever the Content-Type header or the `dataType` specified. For example if the Content-Type header is "application/json" or if you set `dataType` to json then the first converter to be called is text to json.

The general principle is that either the inferred or specified data type makes jQuery call the appropriate converter function.

## Converters

You can specify your own converter functions using the converters option. This is set to an object of key value pairs. The key is the name of the data type to convert between  and the value is the conversion function. By default it is set to:

```
{ "* text": window.String,
  "text html": true,
  "text json": jQuery.parseJSON,
  "text xml": jQuery.parseXML
}
```

any key value pairs that you set via the converters option are added to the defaults – but you can override them. The converter function that you specify

161

has to accept the raw data from the AJAX request and return the processed data.

The best way to understand converters is to first override an existing converter function. As an example let's add date handling to JSON which is a very common real application of converters.

When you convert an object to a JSON string, the conversion handles strings, arrays, numeric values and so on but it doesn't handle dates. A date object simply gets converted to a date string and when jQuery does an automatic conversion the date field is just a string.

For example:

```php
<?php
header("Content-Type:application/json;charset=UTF-8");
$cdata='{"first": "Ian","last":"Elliot",
        "bday":"2013-10-21T13:28:06.419Z"}';
echo($cdata);
?>
```

where the JSON string being sent has a final property bday that is the standard JavaScript string representation of a date/time.

For example if you do:

```javascript
var date = new Date();
var json = JSON.stringify(date);
```

then json will contain something like the string "2013-10-21T13:28:06.419Z".

When you ask for this JSON data using the usual:

```javascript
var options={};
options.url="process.php";
options.method="get";
$.ajax(options).then(
                function(data,test,XHR){
                    console.log(data);
                    });
```

then the data will contain an object:

```
Object { first: "Ian", last: "Elliot",
        bday: "2013-10-21T13:28:06.419Z" }
```

Notice that the bday property is set to a string not a Date object.

If you want to convert bday to a Date object automatically then you can do it by overriding the text to json converter. All you have to do is set the converter's property accordingly:

```
var options={};
options.url="process.php";
options.method="get";
options.converters={
  "text json":function(data){
             data=JSON.parse(data);
             data.bday=new Date(data.bday);
             return data;
           }};

$.ajax(options).then(
             function(data){
                console.log(data);
             });
```

Notice that the custom converter's key is "text json". This means it will be called whenever the Content-Type header or the `dataType` is json to convert the raw text to JSON. The actual function doesn't do a great deal. It gets the raw text in its data parameter and then uses the JSON parser to convert the text to JSON but with bday set to a String. To convert this to a Date we simply create a new Date object using the date string to initialize it. If you try this out you will see:

```
Object { first: "Ian", last: "Elliot",
        bday: Date 2013-10-21T13:28:06.419Z }
```

You can see that the bday property is now a Date object set to the correct date.

## Custom Types and Converters

As well as overriding existing data types you can introduce your own.

For example, in the case of JSON with dates, it is probably a good idea to distinguish your custom JSON format from all other JSON formats. Let's call your particular JSON with date mytype.

What we need now is a converter from text to mytype and this is just the converter we already have but with text mytype as the key:

```
options.converters={"text mytype":
                         function(data){
                    data=JSON.parse(data);
                    data.bday=new Date(data.bday);
                    return data;
                    }
                };
```

Of course, if the server sends the standard json header our converter will not be called so we need to either change the header or set the `dataType` to mytype. If you try the program with:

```
options.dataType="mytype";
```

You will discover that it works perfectly and the converter is called to process the text to mytype conversion even though the server says its just plain ordinary json within its header.

However, if you get the server to send an appropriate header:

```
<?php
header("Content-Type:mytype; charset=UTF-8");
$cdata='{"first": "Ian","last":"Elliot",
        "bday":"2013-10-21T13:28:06.419Z"}';
echo($cdata);
?>
```

You will discover that nothing happens and your custom converter from text to mytype isn't called.

The reason is that mytype is the internal jQuery name for the data type and not the Content-type header that identifies the data type. For example, internally we use the jQuery data type json, but the header that is sent is application/json. Clearly we need to connect the internal name to the header and this is where the mysterious contents option comes into play.

## contents

Is a set of key value pairs. The key is the internal jQuery data type name and the value is a regular expression that matches the header of the type.

So if we want a header that contains mytype to map to the internal jQuery mytype we have to add:

```
options.contents={mytype:/mytype/};
```

Now everything works and the convert is called if the header contains the string mytype.

Notice that you don't have to use the same internal type name and header type name. For example, you could decide to call your data type jsond - for json with dates - and in this case the contents option would be:

```
options.contents={jsond:/mytype/};
```

This works, but if you go to the next step and decide that you really want the header to be jsond as well then you need to use:

```
options.contents={jsond:/jsond/};
```

and you will find that everything stops working.

The reason is very simple. The default for contents is:

```
contents: { xml: /xml/,
            html: /html/,
            json: /json/ }
```

and your key value pair is added to the end of the default list. You can guess what happens. When the server sends a header with jsond in it the entry json:/json/ matches before your jsond:/jsond/ does and so your custom converter never gets called.

There are two possible solutions. Don't call your data type anything like xml, html or json, or modify the definition of json.

For example:

```
options.contents= {jsond:/jsond/,json:/json(?!d)/};
```

This redefines the mapping of json to "json" not followed by "d". In other words the regular expression for json has been modified to only match anything containing "json" but not if it is "jsond". If you now try the program you will find it all works:

```php
<?php
header("Content-Type:jsond; charset=UTF-8");
$cdata='{"first": "Ian","last":"Elliot",
        "bday":"2013-10-21T13:28:06.419Z"}';
echo($cdata);
?>
var options={};
options.url="process.php";
options.method="get";
options.contents={jsond:/jsond/,json:/json(?!d)/};
options.converters={"text jsond":
                            function(data){
                               data=JSON.parse(data);
                               data.bday=new Date(data.bday);
                               return data;
                            }
                  };

$.ajax(options).then(
                function(data){
                   console.log(data);
                });
```

Of course you can still override the header using the dataType option.

## An alternative multi-step approach

If you are implementing a completely new data type then creating a new text to newtype converter and registering a suitable header seems reasonable. However, if what you have is a modification to an existing data type then perhaps a two or even multi-stage process is better.

For example, jsond is just a development of JSON so why not accept JSON, allow jQuery to process it and then convert it to jsonp.

For example, if the server sends a standard JSON header:

```php
<?php
header("Content-Type:application/json;charset=UTF-8");
$cdata='{"first": "Ian","last":"Elliot",
        "bday": "2013-10-21T13:28:06.419Z"}';
echo($cdata);
?>
```

You can allow jQuery to perform the conversion to JSON and then create a converter from json to jsond:

```javascript
var options={};
options.url="process.php";
options.method="get";
options.dataType="jsond";
options.converters={"json jsond":
                    function(data){
                      data.bday=new Date(data.bday);
                      return data;
                    }
                };

$.ajax(options).then(
            function(data){
              console.log(data);
            });
```

Notice that now the dataType is jsond and we don't have to register a new header for the type. Also notice that the converter is now json to jsond rather than text to jsond. With these changes jQuery automatically calls its own text to json converter and then calls the json to jsond converter. Notice that you don't have to explicitly convert the text data to JSON.

If you don't want to rely on the header from the server you could write the dataType as:

```
options.dataType="json jsond";
```

which forces the conversion sequence text->json->jsond no matter what the headers are.

**To summarize:**

- you can create a custom data type by defining converter functions that convert text to your new data type.
- if you want jQuery to recognize a Content-Type header for your new data type you have to define a mapping from the new data type name to the specific header using a regular expression.
- Be careful that your regular expression isn't invalidated by an earlier expression that matches everything your's does.
- You can override existing data type converters in the same way.
- You can extend data type converters by chaining data types in the dataType option – the converters are called in the specified sequence.

# The dataFilter

There is one final function that you can place into jQuery's processing pipeline – the dataFilter. This is a function that is called right after the raw data has been received. The function is passed the raw data as its first parameter and the dataType specified as the second parameter. The function returns the raw data modified as required.

For example, to include a dataFilter in the previous data converter program:

```
var options={};
options.url="process.php";
options.method="get";
options.dataType="json jsond";
options.dataFilter=function(data,datatype){
                    console.log(data);
                    console.log(datatype);
                    return data;
                };
options.converters={"json jsond":
                        function(data){
                          data.bday=new Date(data.bday);
                          return data;
                        }
                    };
$.ajax(options).then(
                function(data){
                  console.log(data);
                });
```

167

If you run this program with the PHP file given in the previous section as the server then you will see:

```
{"first": "Ian","last":"Elliot",
    "bday":"2013-10-21T13:28:06.419Z"}
index.php:55:2
json jsond
```

Which is the raw JSON string and the data type as set by the dataType option.

The idea is that you use the dataFilter to "sanitize" or otherwise modify the raw data received before it is passed on to the converters.

# Summary

- You can use `accepts` to indicate the  type of data the client wants back from the server as indicated in the Accept request header and `dataType` to set the type of data the client expects back from the server – a selection of xml, html, script, json, jsonp or text.

-  Html data is returned as a String.

- Script from the same origin is downloaded as text and then executed.

- json is converted to suitable JavaScript objects with some limitations.

- xml is converted to an XML object.

- You can create your own type converters which take one type to another. These are registered using options.converters.

- You can create your own custom types but these have to be connected to the types specified in the headers returned by the server using the contents option.

- Type converters can be chained so that they are automatically called to convert one type into another. For example text to json followed by json to jsond.

- There is also a data filter function which is called before any of the converters. This is specified using the dataFilter option.

# Chapter 12

# Transports And JSONP

One of the interesting things about jQuery's approach to AJAX is that it can be extended in many ways. In the previous chapter we discovered that you can use converters to create your own data types, but jQuery lets you go much further – you can create your own custom transport types.

AJAX was originally about getting data into a web page without reloading the page using the built-in XMLHttpRequest object that all browsers support. This is generally what is meant when a programmer says that they are using AJAX, but there are other ways of getting data to and from the server, and jQuery attempts to unify all of these ways in a single approach.

The most common alternative transport types provided as standard by jQuery are JSONP and cross domain script. These data types are implemented using a script tag transport, but as they are presented in the same way as the other data types in jQuery AJAX this fact is often overlooked. Let's find out how it works.

## Working with script transport

As explained in the previous chapter, when you make a script AJAX request to the same domain as the page was loaded from, the standard AJAX XMLHttpRequest transport is used. The text that is returned is converted to script using the built-in data type converter:

```
options.contents={script: /(?:java|ecma)script/}
options.converters={"text script":
                    function( text ) {
                       jQuery.globalEval( text );
                       return text;
                    }
             }
```

Notice that this causes the script to be evaluated and the text returned for further processing. The advantage of using the XMLHttpRequest transport is that all of the status indicators, events and errors are generated automatically.

However, the XMLHttpRequest transport doesn't work with a cross domain request (without the help of CORS). If you make a cross domain script request then jQuery switches to a different transport that does work across domains.

A cross domain script request is quite different from the majority of jQuery AJAX requests. It isn't implemented using the built-in XMLHttpRequest object. Instead the request is made by dynamically adding a <script> tag to the DOM with the URL of the requested script. Doing this automatically starts the browser downloading the script and then executing it when loaded.

For example, when you make a request for a script data type what jQuery actually does is:

```
script = document.createElement('script');
script.type = 'text/javascript';
script.src = 'http://myScript.js';
```

As soon as the src property is set the browser starts to download the specified script. When the script has been downloaded it is added to the script DOM element and executed.

There are differences in the two types of transport. For example the only error that you will get is a time out and there is no returned raw data for a script transport.

You can force jQuery to use a cross domain transport using the crossDomain option;

### crossDomain

If you want jQuery to treat a request as cross domain even when it isn't, you can set crossDomain to true. This will result in any cross domain alternative transport to be used in place of the XMLHttpRequest transport.

For example, if you want to make a cross domain script request to the same domain that the page was served from you could use:

```
var options={};
options.url="process.php";
options.method="get";
options.dataType="script";
options.crossDomain=true;
$.ajax(options).then(
                function(data){
                   console.log(data);
                });
```

In this case the script will be loaded and executed and the done method will be called but data will be undefined.

## Working with JSONP transport

JSONP is a variant of Script transport. It sends JSON formatted data but wrapped by a function call which is executed to process the data. The function is supplied by the client.

So put simply a JSONP request is a Script request where the script has the standard format:

```
wrapperFunction(JSON);
```

As in the case of a Script request, which transport is used depends on whether the domain of the request is the same as the page or different.

If the request is to the same domain then the XMLHttpRequest transport is used and the same basic data conversions are used as for Script. That is the JSONP is downloaded as text and then converted to Script and executed.

If you make a cross domain JSONP request, or indeed a cross domain JSON request, then jQuery automatically switches to using the Script transport. There are a few differences but in the main you can assume that JSONP works in roughly the same way no matter what the transport is, and this isn't quite the same as jQuery AJAX in the case of other data types.

Why would we bother to implement JSON data transfer in this roundabout way?

Why not just use JSON?

The simple answer is that an XMLHttpRequest cannot be to anything other than the domain the page making the request was loaded from, unless you make use of CORs – see later. A script based transport, on the other hand can work cross domain by default. By wrapping the JSON data in a function call we convert the data into a script that can be executed and hence something that can make use of script transport for cross domain requests.

That is, you can use JSONP to retrieve JSON data from any server that supports it without the problem of the same domain policy.

That is, there are a few additional mechanisms that relate to the wrapper function that you need to know about to make use of JSONP.

As already explained, if you make a JSONP request the code is downloaded and run. By convention this code is usually a single function which is passed the JSON string:

```
myFunction(jsonData);
```

When this is loaded and executed then myFunction is run on the client and as already explained myFunction is provided by the client and not as part of the JSONP code.

This provides a callback mechanism in that you can define myFunction to process the jsonData in any way that you like and the calling of myFunction indicates that the JSONP request has been completed i.e. the JSON data is ready to work with.

Of course the client and the server have to agree on the name of the function to be used and this makes the protocol just a little more complicated.

The way that JSONP is implemented introduces some differences in the general AJAX handling that go beyond just a simple change in transport.

The first big difference is that jQuery cannot effectively work with JSONP unless you explicitly tell it that you are making a JSONP request, because it needs to set things up correctly before the request is made. That is, for the JSONP script tag mechanism to be used you have to set dataType to jsonp.

The second big difference is that unless you play by some additional rules you will not be able to make use of the Promise based callbacks or indeed any of the usual AJAX callbacks. The reason is that to make JSONP look like a standard AJAX request jQuery maps the function that wraps the JSON data to the success method of the Promise object.

It is instructive to first see how this all works if you don't play by these additional rules.

Let's make a very simple "raw" JSONP request:

```
var options={};
options.url="process.php";
options.method="get";
options.dataType="jsonp";
$.ajax(options).done(
                function(data){
                   console.log(data);
                });
```

Even at this basic level there is already a new "rule" in operation – you have to use a get and not a post. The reason is that jQuery adds some data to the Get URL that we will have to make use of later.

## Serverside

At the server the only task is to wrap some JSON in a function wrapper and return the result as if it was a script:

```
<?php
header("Content-Type:application/javascript;charset=UTF-8");
$json='{"first": "Ian","last":"Elliot"}';
$cdata="myFunction('".$json."');";
echo($cdata);
?>
```

If you try this out you will be disappointed to discover that nothing works.

The AJAX then function is never called because jQuery uses a different method to detect the completion of a JSONP request.

When the script is run it attempts to call myFunction with the JSON data, but of course there is no myFunction. We can remedy this by adding a myFunction to our client side program:

```
function myFunction(data){
 console.log(data);
};
```

Now when you run the program you will see the JSON string in the console.

```
{"first": "Ian","last":"Elliot"}
```

Again the AJAX request never seems to complete and again this is because we haven't supplied the sort of wrapper function that jQuery expects.

To know that the JSONP request has completed jQuery has to "know" the name of the wrapper function.

if you set the jsonpCallback option to the name of the wrapper function:

## jsonpCallback

Sets the name of the callback function that the server wraps the JSON data in and is implemented in the client.

For example if you add:

```
options.jsonpCallback= "myFunction";
```

then jQuery will hook into myFunction and fire the Promise object's done method when it runs.

Now if you run the program you will see the JSON string twice – once from the myFunction wrapper and once from the AJAX done method. This works no matter which of the two transports is used.

We can even avoid having to define an explicit wrapper function within the client. Instead you can get jQuery to pass the name of a suitable wrapper function to the server by simply not specifying a callback. By default jQuery will add a query string callback=long random number. It also creates a callback function with the same random name that simply calls the then method as if an AJAX call had just completed.

Of course to make this work the server has to add a wrapper function with the name specified by the client – but this is easy:

```
<?php
header("Content-Type:application/javascript;charset=UTF-8");
$callback = $_GET["callback"];
$json='{"first": "Ian","last":"Elliot"}';
$cdata=$callback."('".$json."');";
echo($cdata);
?>
```

All that happens differently is that now the server retrieves the query string and uses it as the name of the function to wrap the JSON. Now if you run the client:

```
var options={};
options.url="process.php";
options.method="get";
options.dataType="jsonp";
$.ajax(options).done(
                function(data){
                  console.log(data);
                });
```

then you will see the JSON data in the console just as if this was a standard AJAX call.

If you want to take more control of the transaction then you might need to specify the jsonp option to change the name of the query string passed to the server.

### jsonp

Sets the name of the key passed to the server value of the callback name within the URL.

So for example if the server wants a query string called jsonRequest you can make the client send it using:

```
options.jsonp="jsonRequest";
```

Now the client will send jsonRequest=some random number to the server and of course the server has to get the jsonRequest parameter:

```
$callback = $_GET["jsonRequest"];
```

You can also stop jQuery sending any callback parameter by setting jsonp to false.

In this case you do need to set jsonpCallback to the name of the callback wrapper function or you have to remember to provide your own function in the client code.

To summarize:

- A JSONP request will use the XMLHttpRequest transport for a same domain request, and a Script transport for a cross domain request.
- If you are writing your own server side code then simply let jQuery generate a name for the wrapper function. Make the server wrap the JSON with a function as specified in the callback parameter and don't implement anything on the client side. You can treat the whole interaction as if it was an AJAX call with the JSON data delivered to the then method as usual.

- If you have to write a client to work with a server that has already been set up to use a specific wrapper name then specify the jsonpCallback option to set the name of the wrapper function that the server uses.

- If the server has been set up to wrap the JSON in a function specified by some other parameter use the jsonp option to specify the name of the parameter.

A couple of final points.

If you make a cross domain request then script transport is used and you will not get the same range of error handling.

Cross domain JSONP is an inherent security risk because you are relying on the server not to return any dangerous code.

## Custom transport

The idea that jQuery can use different transports to implement an AJAX request is a powerful one. You can add your own transports to jQuery very easily – however, implementing the new transport on the server is usually more difficult.

To add a new transport to jQuery all you have to do is use the ajaxTransport method.

### ajaxTransport(dataType,handler)

Adds a new transport method for the named data type.

The only complicated part about ajaxTransport is that the function that you specify as the second parameter doesn't implement the transport, it simply returns an object that does i.e. it is a transport object factory.

The definition of the transport object factory is:

```
function(options,originalOptions,jqXHR)
```

where options are the request options including any defaults, originalOptions are the options explicitly set by the user, and jqXHR is the jqXHR object constructed for the request. The jqXHR object has a lot of additional information about the request including the url etc.

The transport object factory has to return a transport object which has just two methods send and abort:

```
send :function(headers,completeCallback)
```

This just has to implement the transport and call completeCallback when the transport is completed. It can use the headers passed into the function as necessary.

```
abort :function()
```

This simply has to abort the transport – which is often easier said than done!

The final function to define in this set is completeCallback:

```
function(status,statusText,responses,headers)
```

Where status and statusText give the response code and text, responses is a set of dataType key value pairs i.e. it is the payload of the transport, and headers is again a set of optional response headers.

Let's implement the simplest example of a new transport which returns a fixed string immediately.

The transport object factory is:

```
function myTransportFactory(options,originalOptions,jqXHR){
 var transport={
    send:function(headers,callback){
         callback(200,"success"{mydatatype:"this is the data"});
         },
    abort:function(){
         }
    };
 return transport;
}
```

Notice that all this does is to construct an object with two properties send and abort. The send function calls the callback function to signal that it is complete at once. It sends back the success status code and text and the data "this is the data". Notice that the data type has to be the type that the transport is designed to handle otherwise a converter will be called.

To register the new transport all we have to do is:

```
$.ajaxTransport("mydatatype",myTransportFactory);
```

The entire program is:

```
$.ajaxTransport("mydatatype",myTransportFactory);
var options={};
options.url="process.php";
options.method="get";
options.dataType="mydatatype";
$.ajax(options).then(
                function(data){
                  console.log(data);
                });
```

In this case the url and the method are fairly irrelevant. Notice that the datatype has to be mydatatype. If the transport returns alternative data types then you might need a converter. If you run the program you should see "this is the data" in the console.

Now that you have seen a simple example you are probably wondering what sorts of things you could implement using a custom transport. The first thing to notice is that you could use the simple example as a testing harness for AJAX programs so it isn't completely useless.

## Image Transport

Until recently there haven't been many options for new transports because there aren't many different ways of starting a data transfer in a browser. The two best known are the image tag transport and the hidden frame download. You can find jQuery plugins for both types of transport. Today you also have the option of using sockets to implement any transport you care to invent.

Although the documentation gives an example of an image transport, it is worth providing a simpler implementation so that you can see how a real transport might be created. The reason that this implementation is simpler is that it does no error handling.

The transport object factory is simply:

```
function myTransportFactory(options,originalOptions,jqXHR){
 var myimage;
 var transport={
   send:function(headers,callback){
         myimage=new Image();
         myimage.onload=function(){
                          callback(200,"success",{image:myimage});
                       };
         myimage.src=options.url;
       },

   abort:function(){
         myimage=null;
       }
   };
 return transport;
}
```

This follows the same outline as the previous example. It creates an Image object, sets its onload event handler and then starts it downloading by setting its src property to the url. Notice that when the Image has loaded, the onload function simply calls the callback with the image.

To use this new transport you would write something like:

```
$.ajaxTransport("image",myTransportFactory);
var options={};
options.url="test.jpg";
options.method="get";
options.dataType="image";

$.ajax(options).then(
                function(data){
                  $("body").append(data);
                  console.log(data);
                });
```

After registering the transport factory to handle the image type, the AJAX request is set up and the url is set to test.jpg. When the file is loaded the Image object is added to the DOM in the done method.

If you run this program then you will see the image appear in the web page and you will see an image tag displayed in the console.

To make this into something more robust you would have to add error handling.

## Custom prefilters

You can do most of the things that you need to with a custom transport but sometimes you need to modify the way things are set up before the transport is invoked. For example, in the case of the JSONP transport it is necessary to set up the wrapper function before the transport is called to load and run the script.

To allow you to modify things before the transport is put into action you can create a custom prefilter. If you have read the section on creating a custom transport then the general outline of what is to follow will be familiar. To register a prefilter for a particular data type you would use the ajaxPrefilter method.

### ajaxPrefilter(dataTypes,handler)

The handler is a function that will be called for the specified datatypes before the appropriate transport is invoked.

Notice that unlike the transport the handler is the function that is called. The handler is:

```
function handler(options, originalOptions,jqXHR)
```

Where the parameters are the same as in the transport registration – options, the options for the call including defaults, originalOptions – the options explicitly set by the user and the jqXHR object generated by the request. The handler can also return a datatype if the request is better handled as a completely different data type. This is what the JSONP prefilter does, it sets up the wrapper function and then returns "script" so that the Script prefilter, transport, converters etc are used after the prefilter has set everything up correctly.

For example, if you want to do a task before the image transport is called you could use:

```
$.ajaxPrefilter("image",
                function(options,originalOptions,jqXHR){
                  console.log("prefilter");
                });
```

Of course code that you put in the prefilter could have been put into the start of the transport object, assuming that there is a custom transport object. If the prefilter can set things up and then hand off to an existing transport then it is worth using a prefilter. Similarly, if a prefilter can be used with more than one data type or more than one transport then it is better to write a single prefilter function than to put the same code into each of the data types or transport objects.

# Summary

- Script transport is handled differently depending on whether it is a same site or cross site request. For a same site request the script is downloaded as text and executed. For a cross site request the script is added to the DOM and the browser deals with it.

- JSONP is a way to download data possibly cross site by converting it into a script request.

- A JSONP request will use the XMLHttpRequest transport for a same domain request and a script transport for a cross domain request.

- If you are writing your own server side code then simply let jQuery generate a name for the wrapper function. Make the server wrap the JSON with a function as specified in the callback parameter and don't implement anything on the client side. You can treat the whole interaction as if it was an AJAX call with the JSON data delivered to the then method as usual.

- If you have to write a client to work with a server that has already been set up to use a specific wrapper name then specify the jsonpCallback option to set the name of the wrapper function that the server uses.

- If the server has been set up to wrap the JSON in a function specified by some other parameter use the jsonp option to specify the name of the parameter.

- You can implement your own transport using the ajaxTransport function.

- A prefilter function can also be specified which is called before the transport function.

# Chapter 13
# The jqXHR Object

The jQuery approach to AJAX is built on the jqXHR object which wraps the XmlHttpRequest object that the browser provides. It isn't often that you need delve this deeply into jQuery AJAX, but when you do nothing else will do.

## The jqXHR Object

The jqXHR object, or jq(uery)XmlHttpRequest object, is one of the low level features of using jQuery AJAX that at first can mostly be ignored. However, it keeps popping up as it is passed in as a parameter to most of the AJAX event handlers and Promise methods. When you first start using jQuery AJAX you can just treat it as an object that has a number of useful properties that tell you about the nature of the request.

In fact, the jqXHR object is a wrapper for the native XMLHttpRequest object that the browser creates to make an AJAX request. It isn't just a wrapper, it extends the native object where necessary and stands in for it when a transport is used that isn't based on the XMLHttpRequest object.

This is an important point because AJAX proper is based on the XMLHttpRequest object that the browser provides and this implements the HTTP transport needed between the client and the server. However, as we saw in the previous chapter jQuery can make use of other more general transport objects which are not strictly AJAX and certainly don't make use of the browser's XMLHttpRequest object. In this case the transport has to create a jqXHR object that provides as many properties and methods as possible.

In addition to wrapping the XMLHttpRequest object, the jqXHR object is also a Promise which means it can be used to handle asynchronous requests more logically.

An older set of methods – success, error and complete are still supported but don't use them as they are being deprecated – see later for more details.

The jqXHR object also provides the following properties and methods:

- readyState

| 0 | UNSENT | The connection has not started |
|---|---|---|
| 1 | OPENED | The data is sent |
| 2 | HEADERS_RECEIVED | headers and status are available. |
| 3 | LOADING | Downloading; responseText holds partial data. |
| 4 | DONE | The operation is complete. |

- **status**
  The HTTP result code.

- **statusText**
  The HTTP result text.

- **responseXML** and/or **responseTex**t when the underlying request responded with xml and/or text, respectively.

- **setRequestHeader**(name, value)
  replaces the named header with the value given. This can only be used from the beforeSend function - see later.

- **getAllResponseHeaders**()
  Returns a single string with all of the headers.

- **overrideMimeType**()
  overrides the mimetype header. This can only be used in the beforeSend function.

- **getResponseHeader**(name)
  returns a string with the named header.

- **statusCode**()
  This can be used to set callbacks for any HTTP result code. It has to be set in the beforeSend function – see later.

- **abort**()
  Aborts the transfer – if this is possible.

If you look at the specification of the native XMLHttpRequest object you will discover that it has many more advanced options. However, these are not supported by the jqXHR object because they do not work on all browsers. The list of properties and methods is likely to expand as the newer features spread to the majority of browsers.

However, if you want to try to set a field on the native XMLHttpRequest you can use the xhrFields option.

### xhrField=object of key value pairs

sets the fields named as keys in the object to the value specified.

For example:

```
options.xhrFields={"timeout",1000);
```

sets the timeout field to 1000 ms. In most cases you should use the option provided by jQuery rather than setting the native field, but this is useful if you need to modify any non-standard fields.

If you really want to do advanced things you can even make use of the xhr option to provide a function that will create a custom XMLHttpRequest object.

### xhr=function()

Set to a function that returns a custom XMLHttpRequest object.

In most cases this is only useful in creating an enhanced native XMLHttpRequest object.

One of the confusing aspects of the jqXHR object is that many of its properties and methods are available as options in the main AJAX function call.

In most cases which you use is a matter of convenience and preference and, most importantly, exactly where in the AJAX request the actions are carried out. Setting jqXHR properties and using its methods generally happens at a later stage in the request and therefore tends to override what has been set using the AJAX request options.

## AjaxSetup

As well as being able to set options when you make an AJAX call you can also pre-specify all of the options as defaults using the AjaxSetup method.

For example:

```
$.ajaxSetup({ url:"mysite.com"})
```

sets the default for the url property to mysite.com. Now if an AJAX call, any AJAX call, is started without an explicit url option it will request data from mysite.com.

That is you can set defaults for all AJAX options which apply to all AJAX methods – ajax, get, post etc. - unless they are overridden by explicit option values.

The jQuery documentation argues that this isn't a good idea because it might change the way that AJAX requests are handled from third party plugins and so on but sometimes this is what you want to do. So rather then avoiding the use of ajaxSetup you should consider very carefully how to use it. Always specify every option that your AJAX call relies on and don't simply accept defaults that you might later change.

Normally any defaults you set using ajaxSetup can be overridden by explicitly set options at the time of the call – however using beforeSend and the jqXHR object you can enforce many of the defaults – as explained in the next section

## beforeSend

```
beforeSend=function(jqXHR,options)
```

Called just before the AJAX transport is started so that you can modify any aspect of the request.

You can change the properties of the jqXHR object any time you have access to it but often you need to add code to the beforeSend function to modify it just before the AJAX request gets underway i.e. when jqXHR.readyState==0.

Notice that at this early stage many of the properties and methods that use data set by the response are either null or undefined. For example, if you try to access say status or statusText you will find they are undefined.

One reason for using the beforeSend function it to modify options and jqXHR properties after they have been set by the AJAX call. For example:

```
options.beforeSend=function(jqXHR,options){
                options.url="process.php";
        };
```

sets the url property to "process.php" no matter what the AJAX request originally asked for.

Using the beforeSend function you can override any choices made at the AJAX call by setting them later in the request sequence. By setting beforeSend in ajaxSetup you can enforce your choices for all AJAX requests without having to set it as part of the options in each AJAX call:

```
$.ajaxSetup({
        beforeSend:function(jqXHR,options){
                options.url="process.php";
            }
        }
```

The beforeSend approach has a number of common applications which we'll now explore.

## Custom Headers

Typical uses of beforeSend are to set any request headers you might need. For example:

```
options.beforeSend=function(jqXHR,settings){
                jqXHR.setRequestHeader('myHeader', 'myValue');
                };
```

If you examine the headers at the server – try:

```
$headers = getallheaders();
foreach($headers as $key=>$val){
 echo $key . ': ' . $val . '<br>';
}
```

you will find that there is a new header:

```
myHeader: myValue
```

You can also specify a header or set of headers using the options. It can be done in the headers option. for example

```
options.headers={'myHeader','myValue'};
```

sets the same custom header.

The only difference between the two methods is perhaps visibility to the programmer working at a higher level. If you use the beforeSend function then the setting of the header is slightly less visible than the options method. It also overrides any header set in the options.

There are lot of reasons for setting custom headers. One major reason is to perform cross domain requests using CORS. As this involves the server to a great extent it is beyond the scope of this chapter -

Another common use of custom headers is to send a user name and password as part of HTTP authentication. To make things easier in this case jQuery provides the username and password options which can be set to the appropriate user name and password and automatically generated the necessary authentication headers.

## Setting HTTP code handlers.

There is a facility in jQuery to define handlers that are automatically called according to the HTTP code returned by the server. You can, of course use the jqXHR status property and an if statement within the done or fail methods to explicitly call status code handlers but if you register a status code handler using the **statusCode** function it will be called automatically.  For example,

```
options.beforeSend=function(jqXHR,settings){
                    jqXHR.statusCode({404:
                            function(data, textStatus, jqXHR){
                              console.log("status 404");
                              console.log(textStatus);
                            }
                          });
                }
```

This passed to the statusCode function a map of key value pairs. In this case the value is the HTTP code and the value is the function to be called when that HTTP code is returned.

You can achieve exactly the same result using the statusCode option:

```
options.statusCode={404:
   function(data, textStatus, jqXHR){
     console.log("status 404");
     console.log(textStatus);
   }
 }
```

Again which one is best to use depends on at what point in the request you want to attach the handlers.

## The Local and Global Event Handlers

In most cases you only need to make use of the Promise that the ajax method returns to handle the result of an AJAX request. However before the use of the Promise object there were and still are the old event handlers.

These are deprecated and you shouldn't use them if at all possible but you might need to know about them:

 ◆  success is the same as the Promise done method

 ◆  error is the same as the Promise fail method

 ◆  complete is the same  as the Promise always method

The call sequence of all of the event handlers is:

```
beforeSend
request started
 .   .   .
response received
if fail then
 error
 Promise fail
else
 dataFilter
 success
 Promise done
 Promise complete
```

Notice that the Promise methods can have multiple handlers assigned to them and they will all be executed and in the order that they were defined. The old event handlers can only have a single function to execute.

As well as these "local" events there are also global event handlers that can be set to apply to all AJAX requests.

However it is important to note that global event handlers are never invoked during a JSONP or a cross domain script request as these do not use the XmlHttpRequest object for transport.

All of the global handlers accept an event handler with the same form:

```
function(event,jqXHR,options)
```

They all also have to be attached to the document object.

The relationship between the global and local events is well described in the documentation:

- **ajaxStart** (Global Event)
  This event is triggered if an AJAX request is started and no other AJAX requests are currently running.

- **beforeSend** (Local Event)
  This event, which is triggered before an AJAX request is started.

- **ajaxSend** (Global Event)
  This global event is also triggered before the request is run.

- **success** (Local Event)
  This event is only called if the request was successful (no errors from the server, no errors with the data).

- **ajaxSuccess** (Global Event)
  This event is also only called if the request was successful.

- **error** (Local Event)
  This event is only called if an error occurred with the request (you can never have both an error and a success callback with a request).

- ◆ **ajaxError** (Global Event)
  This global event behaves the same as the local error event.

- ◆ **complete** (Local Event)
  This event is called regardless of if the request was successful, or not. You will always receive a complete callback, even for synchronous requests.

- ◆ **ajaxComplete** (Global Event)
  This event behaves the same as the complete event and will be triggered every time an AJAX request finishes.

- ◆ **ajaxStop** (Global Event)
  This global event is triggered if there are no more AJAX requests being processed.

Notice that the ajaxStart/Stop events can be used to keep track of overall AJAX activity. Apart from this the global events are simply alternatives to the local events.

For example you could use

```
$(document).ajaxSend(
            function(event,jqXHR, options){
                jqXHR.setRequestHeader('myHeader', 'myValue');
            });
```

in place of the beforeSend function.

You can also turn off all global events by setting the **global** option to false.

Finally there is the **context** option. By default in all event handlers and callbacks this is set to object that is the result of merging the options set by ajaxSettings and the options specified in the call. So for example you could use:

```
$.ajaxSetup({
            beforeSend:function(jqXHR,options){
                        this.url="process.php";
                    }
            });
```

in place of options.url.

Alternatively you can set this to any object that might be useful using the context option. For example:

```
options.context=$("body");
```

This sets this to a jQuery object wrapping the portion of the DOM corresponding to the body tag.

After this you can write things like:

```
function(data,test,XHR){
  console.log(this.html());
});
```

Notice that html() is a jQuery method and `this` is a jQuery result object.

This sort of technique is only likely to be useful in situations where you need to change the object that the event handlers/callbacks operate on. In most cases it is easier to do the processing on the object explicitly e.g.

```
function(data,test,jqXHR){
  console.log($("body").html());
});
```

# Summary

- The jqXHR object is a wrapper for the native XMLHttpRequest object that the browser creates to make an AJAX request. It isn't just a wrapper it extends the native object where necessary and stands in for it when a transport is used that isn't based on the XMLHttpRequest object.

- However, if you want to try to set a field on the native XMLHttpRequest you can use the xhrFields option.

- As well as being able to set options when you make an AJAX call you can also pre-specify all of the options as defaults using the AjaxSetup method.

- beforeSend specifies a function called just before the AJAX transport is started so that you can modify any aspect of the request. Typical uses of beforeSend are to set any request headers you might need.

- If you register a status code handler using the statusCode function it will be called automatically if the server returns that code.

- In most cases you only need to make use of the Promise that the ajax method returns. However, before the use of the Promise object there were and still are the old event handlers. These are deprecated and you shouldn't use them if at all possible but you might need to know about them.

# Chapter 14
# Character Encoding

One of the biggest problems you encounter in using AJAX is the dreaded character encoding. No matter what data format you select, the data is actually transmitted as text. But it isn't as simple as this sounds.

Before we start to look at character encoding within AJAX we have to understand the problem it tries to solve. At its most basic, data on the Internet consists of groups of 8-bits known at an "octet" but usually just called a "byte". Obviously to represent character data we need a mapping between numeric values and characters. One of the first standards for this was, and is, ASCII. This defines 127 alphanumeric characters: A-Z; a-z; 0-9; command characters such as carriage return and backspace; and assorted special characters. Of course, using 8 bits you can represent 256 characters, but this isn't enough to represent all of the characters used by even a small selection of the written languages of the world.

## ISO-8859

The first solution to this problem was to simply reuse the same 256 numeric codes and associate them with different sets of characters. The most commonly used on the internet is ISO 8859-$n$ where $n$ is between 1 and 16. Each value of $n$ maps a different set of characters onto the 0 to 255 values that a byte can represent. For example, ISO 8859-1 is Latin-1 Western European and if selected provides characters for most Western European languages. ISO-8859-2 is Latin-2 Central European and provides characters for Bosnian, Polish, Croatian and so on.

Notice that we now have a situation where a single character code can correspond to different characters depending on which ISO-8859 character set is selected. This is the source of problems if a server sends data using one ISO-8859 character set and the browser displays it using another. The data hasn't changed but what is displayed on each system is different. To stop this from happening, servers send a header stating the character set in use.

For example:

```
Content-Type: text/html; charset=ISO-8859-1
```

sets the character set to Latin 1. The problem with this is that the server can't adjust its headers for an individual page. Setting the HTTP header for an entire site is reasonable, but you still might want to send a page in another character set.

To allow this you can use the meta tag:

```
<meta http-equiv="Content-Type" content="text/html;
                        charset=ISO-8859-1">
```

This has to be the first tag in the <head> section because the page cannot be rendered until the browser knows the charset in use. Notice that adding an HTTP header or an HTML meta tag only tells the browser what encoding is in use, it doesn't actually enforce the encoding or convert anything from one encoding to another.

What matters is what encoding the file is stored using. For example, to use ISO-8859-2 when you save a file when using an editor such as Notepad++, select encoding Ansi and character set Eastern European.

The encoding used for the file determines how all of the characters it contains are represented, and this includes string literals used in JavaScript or PHP programs.

## Unicode

Most of what we have just looked at is legacy because the proper way to do character representation today is to use Unicode. However, you will still encounter websites using ISO character sets and you need to understand how they work. By comparison Unicode is more logical and complete. Unicode is just a list of characters indexed by a 32-bit value called the character's code point. There are enough characters in Unicode to represent every language in use and some that aren't.

Unicode defines the characters, but it doesn't say how the code point should be represented. The simplest is to use a 32-bit index for every character. This is UTF-32 and it is simple, but very inefficient. It is roughly four times bigger than ASCII. In practice we use more efficient encodings.

# UTF-8

There are a number of encodings of Unicode, but the most important for the web is UTF-8. There are 1,112,064 characters in UTF-8 and clearly these cannot all be represented by a value in a single byte as the 256 characters of ASCII could. Instead UTF-8 is a variable length code that uses up to four bytes to represent a character.

How many bytes are used to code a character is indicated by the most significant bits of the first byte.

```
Byte 1
0xxxxxxx    one byte
110xxxxx    two bytes
1110xxxx    three bytes
11110xxx    four bytes
```

All subsequent bytes have their most significant two bits set to 10. This means that you can always tell a follow-on byte from a first byte. The bits in the table shown as x carry the information about which character is represented. To get the character code you simply extract the bits and concatenate them to get a 7, 11, 16 or 21-bit character code. Notice that, unlike the ISO schemes, there is only one character assigned to a character code. This means that if the server sends UTF-8 and the browser interprets the data as UTF-8 then there is no ambiguity.

The first 128 characters of UTF-8 are the same as ASCII, so if you use a value less than 128 stored in a single byte then you have backward compatible ASCII text. That is, Unicode characters U+0000 to U+007F can be represented in a single byte. Going beyond this needs two, three and four bytes. Almost all the Latin alphabets plus Greek, Cyrillic, Coptic, Armenian, Hebrew, Arabic, Syrian, Thaana and N'Ko can be represented with just two bytes.

As long as the server sends out a header:

```
Content-Type: text/html; charset=UTF-8
```

or you include:

```
<meta charset="UTF-8">
```

as the first tag in the web page, the browser will interpret the stream of bytes as UTF-8. Nothing can go wrong as long as the server is actually sending UTF-8 encoded text.

One complication is that if the server sends out a header that sets the character coding, this takes precedence over the meta tag. This suggests that if you want to serve pages in different encodings you should set the server not to send out character encoding headers.

195

If you want to include a UTF-8 character that is outside the usual range, i.e. one you cannot type using the default keyboard, then you can enter it using:

`&#decimal;`

or

`&#xhex;`

where decimal and hex are the character codes in decimal and hex. For example:

`&#x2211;`

will display a mathematical summation sign, i.e. a sigma.

$\Sigma$

If you don't see a Greek sigma as above when loaded into a browser then it isn't using HTML5. Many of the common symbols have HTML entity names. For example, you can enter the summation symbol using &sum;.

You also have to be careful about text that is processed by the server. For example, text stored in a database needs to be in the same representation that the server is going to use. Similarly, you have to pay attention to text processed by server-side languages like PHP.

The most important single idea is:

**The browser always works with UTF-8 encoded data and, if it can, will convert any other encoding as the web page is read in.**

To do this it has to know what the encoding is and it has to support converting it.

## UTF-16 in JavaScript

JavaScript has Unicode support and all JavaScript strings are UTF-16 coded – this has some unexpected results for any programmer under the impression that they can assume that one character is one byte. While you can mostly ignore the encoding used, the fact that web pages use UTF-8 and JavaScript uses UTF-16 can cause problems.

**The key idea is that when JavaScript interacts with a web page characters are converted from UTF-8 to UTF-16 and vice versa.**

As you can guess UTF-16 is another variable length way of coding Unicode but as the basic unit is 16 bits we only need to allow for the possibility of an additional two-byte word.

For any Unicode character in the range U+0000 to U+FFFF, i.e. 16 bits, you simply set the single 16-bit word to the code. So how do we detect that two 16-bit words, called a surrogate pair, are needed? The answer is that the range U+D800 to U+DFFF is reserved and doesn't represent any valid character, i.e. they never occur in a valid string. These reserved codes are used to signal a two-word coding. If you have a Unicode character that has a code larger than U+FFFF then you have to convert it into a surrogate pair:

1.  Subtract 0x010000 from it to give a 20-bit number in the range 0x000000 to 0x0FFFFF.

2.  The top 10 bits are added to 0xD800 to give the first 16-bit surrogate in the range 0xD800 to 0xDBFF.

3.  The low 10 bits are added to 0xDC00 to give the second 16-bit surrogate in the same range.

Reconstructing the character code is just the same process in reverse.

If you find a 16-bit value in the range x0800 to xDFFF then it and the next 16-bit value are a surrogate pair. Take 0xD800 from the first and 0xDC00 from the second. Put the two together to make a 20-bit value and add 0x0100000. The only problem is that different machines use different byte orderings - little endian and big endian. To tell which sort of machine you are working with, a Byte Order mark or BOM can be included in a string U+FEFF. If this is read as FFEF the machine doing the decoding has a different byte order to the machine that did the coding.

## The BMP - Basic Multilingual Plane

A JavaScript string usually uses nothing but characters that can be represented in a single 16-bit word in UTF-16. As long as you can restrict yourself to the Basic Multilingual Plane (BMP), as this set is referred to, everything works simply. If you can't, then things become much harder.

You can enter a Unicode character using an escape sequence:

`\xHH`

for characters that have codes up to xFF, i.e. 0 to 255, and:

`\uHHHH`

for characters that have codes up to xFFFF, where H is a hex digit.

For example:

```
var a = "Hello World\u00A9";
console.log(a);
```

adds a copyright symbol to the end of Hello World. This is simple enough, but if you now try:

```
console.log(a.length);
```

you will find that it displays 12, because the length property counts the number of 16-bit characters in a string.

What about the Unicode characters that need two bytes? How can you enter them?

The answer is that in ECMAScript 6 you can enter a 32-bit character code:

\u{HHHHHHHH}

If you cannot assume ECMAScript 6 then you have to enter the surrogate pairs as two characters.

You can easily write a function that will return a UTF-16 encoding of a Unicode character code:

```
function codeToUTF16(code) {
 if (code <= 0xFFFF) return "\\u" + code.toString(16).toUpperCase();
 code = code − 0x10000;
 var sLead = 0xD800 | (code >> 10);
 var sTrail = 0xDC00 | (code & 0x3FF);
 return "\\u" + sLead.toString(16).toUpperCase() +
         "\\u" + sTrail.toString(16).toUpperCase();
}
```

For example:

```
console.log(codeToUTF16(0x1F638));
```

produces:

\uD83D\uDE38

which is the "grinning cat face with smiling eyes".

localhost:8383 says:

If you try to display this on the console the chances are you won't see it – it depends on what is hosting the console. If you show it in an alert then you should see it, as the browser will convert it to UTF-8 and then display it:

```
alert("\uD83D\uDE38");
```

Notice JavaScript sends the UTF-16 to the browser unmodified – it is the browser that converts it to equivalent UTF-8.

# JavaScript Problems

As mentioned, as soon as you use characters outside of the BMP things get complicated. For example:

```
s= "\uD83D\uDE38";
console.log(lengths);
```

reports the length of the string as two. even though only one character is coded.

At the moment most of the JavaScript functions only work when you use characters from the BMP and there is a one-to-one correspondence between 16-bit values and characters. JavaScript may display surrogate pairs correctly, but in general it doesn't process them correctly.  For example, consider the string that represents two cat emoji:

```
s= "\uD83D\uDE38\uD83D\uDE38";
alert(s.charAt(1));
```

The charAt doesn't give you the final cat emoji, but the character corresponding to the first uDE38, which is an illegal Unicode character, i.e. it returns the 16-bit code corresponding to the second 16-bit word rather than the second character.

You also need to know about the string functions that work with Unicode code values.

- ◆ **fromCharCode** and **fromCodePoint** do the same job - convert a character code to a string – however, fromCharCode only works with 16-bit values and not surrogate pairs. fromCodePoint will return a surrogate pair if the code is greater then 0xFFFF.  The only problem is that fromCodePoint was introduced with ECMAScript 2015 and isn't supported in IE or older browsers. A polyfill is available.

- ◆ **charCodeAt** and **codePointAt** will return the character code at a specified position in a string. The charCodeAt function works in 16-bit values and is blind to surrogate pairs. The codePointAt will return a value greater than 0xFFFF is the position is the start of a surrogate pair. Notice, however, that the position is still in terms of 16-bit values and not characters. The codePointAt function was introduced in ECMAScript 2015 and isn't supported in older browsers. A polyfill is available.

There is one final problem that you need to be aware of.

In Unicode a single code always produces the same character, but there may be many characters that look identical. In technical terms you can create the same glyph, i.e. character, in different ways. Unicode supports combining codes which put together multiple characters into a single character. This means that you can often obtain a character with an accent either by selecting a character with an accent or selecting a character without an accent and combining it with the appropriate accent character. The end result is that two Unicode strings can look identical and yet be represented by different codes. This means the two strings won't be treated as being equal and they might not even have the same length. The solution to this problem is to normalize the strings so that characters are always produced in the same way. This is not an easy topic to deal with in general as there are so many possible ways of approaching it.

The whole subject of safely working with Unicode in JavaScript is too large for this chapter. It is important that you know what the problem is and, if you are going to work with characters that need two 16-bit words, or rather if your users are, then you need to look into ways of processing the strings correctly.

## Working With Non-UTF-8 Encodings

Before moving on to the specific topic of AJAX and encoding, let's just look at the way normal web pages are retrieved using a get.

This is a difficult subject because of the many different ways available to deal with the situation. All modern programs, not just servers and browsers, use Unicode.

If they have an option to save data in another encoding then there are two ways they can do the job:

1. Stay with Unicode and just save a file that uses Unicode characters to look like the character set of the encoding.
2. Convert the Unicode to the encoding in question and create a file that really is in the encoding and not just looks like it is in the encoding.

This confusion between the use of the real encoding and the Unicode equivalent character set occurs in servers and browsers. That is, if you specify an encoding of ISO 8859-2 and enter character 0xA3, which is Ł, the character is stored in a file or a web page on disk as character code 0xA3.

When the web server is asked for the file it reads it in and doesn't change the coding and sends it to the browser complete with HTTP headers and/or meta tags that specify that the data is in ISO 8859-2. This causes the browser to read 0xA3, which it knows is the same character as Unicode 0x141 in ISO 8859-2, and converts it accordingly. It is Unicode 0x141 that is displayed in the web page. Also notice that the character is UTF-8 encoded so that in the web page it is represented by two bytes - 0xC5 and 0x81.

So while characters stored in the file are encoded using ISO 8859-2, when they are loaded into the web page they only look as if they are in the ISO 8859-2 character set, but in fact they are being displayed as the equivalent Unicode characters in UTF-8.

**The browser always works with UTF-8 internally.**

You can prove that this is true by writing a JavaScript program that retrieves the character code at the character's location:

```
alert($("#test").text().charCodeAt(0).toString(16));
```

where test is:

```
<div id="test">Ł</div>
```

with the meta tag:

```
<meta http-equiv="Content-Type" content="text/html;
                            charset=ISO-8859-2">
```

It is also important the HTML file is saved in ISO-8859-2 encoding. You can do this if you use Notepad++ say and select encoding Ansi and character set Eastern European. If the file isn't saved in ISO-8859-2 encoding then things just won't work because the meta tag or the header will incorrectly state what the encoding is.

If correctly encoded, the file contains character code 0xA3 between the div tags, but when the alert is displayed the character code shown is 0x141, which is of course the correct UTF-16 encoding.

Even if you are using a different encoding in the web page, the encoding used by the browser is still Unicode. The only thing that setting the charset property does is to govern how the codes stored in the file and received by the browser are converted into Unicode.

If you follow this idea then what do you think the alert box will show when the content of the div is changed to:

```
<div id="test">&#xA3;</div>
```

The character code 0xA3 in ISO 8859-2 is Ł and this is what you might expect to be displayed, but it isn't. The HTML entity &#xA3; represents Unicode character 0xA3, no matter what the charset is. So the web page shows £, which is Unicode character 0xA3, and the alert box shows A3. No conversion to Unicode is performed because it is already considered to be Unicode.

The charset simply controls how the file sent to the browser is treated as it is converted to Unicode in UTF-8 encoding. Once it is converted everything from that point on works as if it had been Unicode from the beginning.

This might sound complicated, but in fact it is a great simplification. It allows you to write your JavaScript programs using Unicode without having to worry what the charset of the web page it is using when it is loaded.

That is, irrespective of the charset encoding, JavaScript always works with a web page that is encoded using Unicode UTF-8 and when it interacts with the page it uses Unicode, but UTF-16 encoded.

If you don't specify an encoding, most browsers will treat the input data as UTF-8 and what you see depends on how non-UTF-8 data can be interpreted as UTF-8.

What you actually see when an ISO or other encoding is treated as UTF-8 depends on whether the code received forms a legal single, double, triple or even quadruple byte UTF-8 code. All ISO characters up to 0x7F are represented accurately as they are shared between encodings. Everything else is illegal except for 0xC2 or 0xC3 followed by a character in the range 0x80 to 0xbf. It is also worth knowing that the replacement character for illegal UTF-8 codes, a question mark in a diamond, is u+FFFD or 0xEF 0xBF 0xBD as a 3-byte UTF-8 encoding.

## AJAX and Encoding from the Server

Now we come to the matter of what happens when you perform an AJAX operation with respect to encodings. We need to consider the situation with respect to a get and a post.

The main thing to remember is that as far as the server is concerned an AJAX get request is the same as a browser get request. The data that the server sends back is therefore the same as for a "normal" browser request  but there are a few differences in how the browser treats the data.

The character encoding used will therefore be whatever is used in the file that is served, but most browsers will not process the HTML in the body of the response to an AJAX request. This means that you cannot rely on specifying the charset in a meta tag. Most browsers will read and honor the charset specified in a header which they do still read and process as part of the HTTP protocol.

Apart from this, the process or retrieving a file using AJAX works the same way as for a file retrieved by a normal browser get. The charset specified in the header is used to convert the data into the correct UTF-8 Unicode.

For example, create a file test.html containing character code 0xA3 twice, which in ISO 8859-2 is ŁŁ. It is also important that the HTML file is saved in ISO-8859-2 encoding. You can do this if you use Notepad++ and select encoding Ansi and character set Eastern European.

Now if you read the file using:

```
var options = {};
options.url = "test.html";
options.method = "get";
$.ajax(options).then(
                function (data) { alert(data); });
```

what you will find is that the characters show as diamonds with question marks.

The reason for this is that the browser is interpreting the code 0xA3 as UTF-8, where it is an illegal character. Even the two bytes taken together are illegal as no 2-byte encoding starts 0xA3.

Also notice that this behavior doesn't change if you change the encoding of the page that the AJAX script is running in. It also doesn't change if you set jQuery's options.dataType to "html" or "text". The default charset is UTF-8 and what matters is what charset is specified for the file being received.

The problem is how to do this. For a normal web page get you can use a meta tag or an HTTP header and things work – although if both are specified the tag takes precedence.

Let's add a meta tag to the file:

```
<meta http-equiv="Content-Type"
        content="text/html; charset=ISO-8859-2">
ŁŁ
```

Of course you could have a complete HTML page stored in the file, but from the point of view of encoding this is all that matters.

If you try this out and load the file using an AJAX get, what you will see depends on the browser. Chrome takes notice of the charset and converts the ISO codes to Unicode. That is, the 0xA3 which it now knows is in ISO 8859-2 is the same character as Unicode 0x141 and this is what it is converted to. With the browser using Unicode 0x141 the correct character is displayed even though it is UTF-8 encoded.

If you try Firefox, Edge or IE 11 you will discover that the character encoding isn't changed and what you see is the replacement character. That is, the page is treated as if it was UTF-8 and the meta tag is ignored.

As mentioned earlier, some browsers do not process the HTML meta tags included in files retrieved using AJAX.

However, if you place the same information in an HTTP header, for example by serving the following PHP file:

```
<?php
header('Content-Type: text/html; charset=ISO-8859-2');
?>
łł
```

then Chrome, Firefox, Edge and IE take notice and convert the ISO codes to Unicode correctly and you see the correct characters.

The same behavior is true of other AJAX methods that return data from the server. The only safe encoding is UTF-8 unless you place Content-Type HTTP headers into the response.

## AJAX and Encoding to the Server

What about data doing to the server using a post or a get?

Even though they use different methods to send the data to the server, in principle both can be set to a particular encoding using the contentType option.

For example:

```
contentType: "application/x-www-form-urlencoded;
                              charset=ISO-8859-15"
```

Things are not simple, however. You can make them simple by using nothing but UTF-8. If you can't you will have to do battle with each of the systems involved in the interaction.

The problem is that there are too many applications involved in a typical AJAX transaction and they all have an opinion on how to deal with the encoding. For example, there is the browser sending the request, the web server receiving the request, Apache say, the language used to receive the request and generate the response PHP say, the web server sending the response and the browser receiving the response. They all can decide what the encoding is and what it should be and they can each therefore make a mess of it. When debugging a charset/encoding problem you have to verify what is received at each of the stages and this can be difficult.

The biggest problem with AJAX and non-UTF-8 encoding is the following statement in the jQuery documentation:

*Note:* The W3C XMLHttpRequest specification dictates that the charset is always UTF-8; specifying another charset will not force the browser to change the encoding.

If you check the most up-to-date documentation you will find no mention that UTF-8 is always to be used but Edge, IE 11, Firefox and Chrome all do use UTF-8.

The best way to see how things can go wrong is by way of an example. If you have a web page with the meta tag:

```
<meta http-equiv="Content-Type" content="text/html;
                               charset=ISO-8859-2">
```

and the program:

```
var sendData={test:"Ł"};

var options = {};
options.url = "phpinfo.php";
options.method = "post";
options.contentType= "application/x-www-form-urlencoded;
                                    charset=ISO-8859-2";
options.data=sendData;
$.ajax(options).then(
               function (data) {
                 alert(data);
               });
```

It is also important that the HTML file is saved in ISO-8859-2 encoding. You can do this if you use Notepad++ say and select encoding Ansi and character set Eastern European.

Notice that in the ajax call we set contentType and then send the data which is encoded as 0xA3 which is Ł in ISO-8859-2 in the web page. What happens is that the web browser converts this string literal as the page is loaded to the correct Unicode character, i.e. 0x141, which is then sent as UTF-8, i.e. the two bytes 0xC5 and 0x81.

This works in the same way even if you change the post to a get. In this case the data is encoded into the query string as %C5%81.

The conversion from ISO-8859-2 to UTF-8 happens because of the meta tag and not the contentType option. As you can easily prove by removing the meta tag and the contentType, it only works with the meta tag. It would also work with an HTTP header because all that matters is that the page is converted from ISO-8859-2 as it is loaded by the browser. The ajax call has nothing to do with it.

The ajax call always sends the data using UTF-8 because this is what is always used within the web page for text.

This means that the data that the server receives and processes is always in UTF-8 and if you want it to work with another encoding you have to write a program to do the conversion on the fly.

## Round Trips

The fact that the data that goes to the server is always UTF-8 has an effect on the data that the server sends back to the browser. This is something we have already examined in terms of using get to retrieve a file, but in the case of a post there is an additional consideration. The data transfer is two-way and there are two sources of data that can be sent back to the client – the data that the client sent and the data the server retrieves or generates.

Data that is generated by the server is very varied and can range from retrieving a file, retrieving data from a database, or using a language such as PHP. In the case of PHP the system is complicated, but very flexible when used with Apache. In PHP, strings are a sequence of bytes and it doesn't make any attempt to change any encoding. If you use a multi-byte encoding then each byte is treated as a character.

There are a set of functions that work with multibyte characters and encodings and these can be used to programmatically generate output to the browser in any of the supported encodings. However, if you don't make any effort to generate particular encodings, then PHP will return any data it receives in the encoding it was received in. It will also send any string literal in the program using the encoding of the file the program is saved in.

For example, if you assume that the file containing the program is saved in ISO-8859-2 encoding, then that is the encoding used for string literals. You can do this if you use Notepad++ and select encoding Ansi and character set Eastern European. So if you have an instruction:

```
echo("Ł");
```

Then 0xA3 is sent to the browser and no attempt to change its encoding is made. When the browser receives this byte it is interpreted as a UTF-8 encoding and shows as a replacement character because, as we have seen many times, it is an illegal code.

If you add a header, remember meta tags are ignored, to the data sent to the browser that defines the charset correctly, you get a slightly different result:

```
header('Content-Type: text/html; charset=ISO-8859-2');
echo("Ł");
```

With this in place, the browser interprets the 0xA3 as an ISO-8859-2 character and replaces it by Unicode x0141 which is the correct character.

Now it looks as if everything works as long as we include an appropriate header in the response, but there is yet another twist.

Consider the data that the server received as part of the post or get. If we assume that the data in the earlier example:

```
var sendData={test:"Ł"};
```

is sent to the server then:

```
echo($_POST["test"]);
```

will display the correct character in the web page without the header. The reason is simply that the data sent to the server is UTF-8 encoded which means test contains 0xC5 0x81 i.e. as far as PHP is concerned it is a two character string. When you send this string back to the browser it is interpreted as UTF-8 and hence the browser displays the correct character.

However, if you add the header defining the charset as ISO-8859, then things go wrong. The data sent to the browser is 0xC5 0x81 as this is what was received. The browser thinks that is an ISO-8859 encoding and 0xC5 is an L with a dash and 0x81 is an undefined character that displays as an open square.

Thus, if you don't include a header, data that is sent to the server is correctly sent back to the client, but data from the server might not be. If you do include the header, the data from the server is correctly sent to the client, but any data originating from the client isn't.

There is nothing you can do to stop the browser sending UTF-8 and encoding to UTF-8 anything it receives.

Trying to work with AJAX with anything other than UTF-8 seems like fighting nature. It can be done, but you will have to do it in code. You can treat UTF-8 as a "transport" encoding and write code on the client or the server to convert to the encoding that you want to work with.

For example, if you want to send the data from the server in ISO-8859 encoding, assuming you are sending a correct ContentType header, and you want to echo data back to the client you need to use:

```
$test=$_POST["test"];
$test=mb_convert_encoding($test,"ISO-8859-2","UTF-8");
echo($test);
```

This converts the UTF-8 string into ISO-8859, which is now echoed back to the client correctly as long as there is an appropriate Content-Type header.

You have to be aware at all times what encoding is being used and make sure you use just one encoding in a single page.

## Conclusion

The whole subject of encodings and web pages is huge, and well beyond the limits of a single chapter. Even a book would fail to cover every possibility.

If you can, opt to work with nothing but UTF-8. This is the only easy route.

Make sure all files are stored in UTF-8 and that all servers, web and database default to UTF-8. If you do this then things are as simple as they can be. If you have to use legacy encodings, then consider converting to UTF-8 before spending a lot of time trying to work with them as they are encoded. There are too many ways that things can go wrong when you change encodings on the fly.

# Summary

- The original ASCII code only defines the basic 127 characters including some control codes. To cater for more language ISO 8859-*n* and similar encodings were developed. These typically use ASCI for values up to 127 and then custom characters for 128 to 255.

- To make sense of an ISO 8859-n encoding you need to know which one is in use to get the right character set.

- Unicode is a list of characters indexed by the codepoint, a 32-bit value. It has enough code points to represent all the world's languages.

- UTF-8 is a Unicode encoding commonly used on the web. It is a multibyte encoding varying from one to four bytes.

- JavaScript uses the UTF-16 encoding which is variable in  length and can have one or two 16-bit words. However, it only handles a single 16-bit word properly and 2-word characters need special treatment.

- You can enter a unicode character using hex escape sequences. Use \xHH for characters that have codes up to xFF i.e. 0 to 255 and \uHHHH for characters that have codes up to xFFFF.

- When JavaScript sends UTF-16 to a browser it is automatically converted to UTF-8 and vice-versa.

- You can set the character encoding to be used via an HTTP header or an HTML meta tag. This doesn't perform any encoding, but simply tells the browser what encoding has been used in the file used to store the web page or however the data was generated.

- If it supports the encoding, the browser will correctly convert the encoding of a web page, as it is loaded, to UTF-8. This means that the JavaScript always interacts with the same UTF-16 codes, irrespective of the indicated encoding.

- For files that are downloaded by AJAX, only Chrome takes any notice of an included HTML meta tag. To ensure that the encoding is converted to UTF-8 correctly you have to use an HTTP header.

- For data that is sent to the server, the page encoding is correctly converted by the browser, when it was loaded, to UTF-8. The ajax call then simply sends this UTF-8 to the server.

- The fact that the data received by the server is always in UTF-8 can cause a problem if it then wants to send data back to the browser in some other encoding. You either have to convert the UTF-8 to the encoding or the encoding to UTF-8.

- It is much simpler to use UTF-8 for everything.

# Index

211

213

www.ingramcontent.com/pod-product-compliance
Lightning Source LLC
LaVergne TN
LVHW062315060326
832902LV00013B/2228